FADED GLORY

FADED GLORY

Presidents Out of Power

James C. Clark

PRAEGER SPECIAL STUDIES • PRAEGER SCIENTIFIC

New York • Philadelphia • Eastbourne, UK
Toronto • Hong Kong • Tokyo • Sydney

Library of Congress Cataloging in Publication Data

Clark, James C., 1947–
    Faded glory.

    Bibliography: p.
    Includes index.
        1.   Presidents—United States—Biography.
    2.   United States—Politics and government.   I.   Title.
    E176.1.C58   1985   973′.09′92   84–18327
    ISBN 0-03-002569-9 (alk. paper)
    ISBN 0-03-002572-9 (pbk. : alk. paper)

To William Edward Clark
and Louise Covington Clark
for their love and patience

Published in 1985 by Praeger Publishers
CBS Educational and Professional Publishing
a Division of CBS Inc.
521 Fifth Avenue, New York, NY 10175 USA

©1985 by Praeger Publishers

56789 052 987654321

Printed in the United States of America
on acid-free paper

Preface

The men who drafted the constitution had their hands full creating the presidency without having to worry about what would become of presidents after they left office. The result has been a mixture of men who died heavily in debt and a few who used their former position to make fortunes.

Some have died in bitterness, failing in attempts to regain the presidency. Only two presidents, William Howard Taft and John Quincy Adams, achieved greater happiness after leaving the White House. Adams served in the House of Representatives and Taft on the Supreme Court. Andrew Johnson, who as president came within one vote of being impeached, had the satisfaction of serving in the U.S. Senate after leaving the White House.

Four presidents tried to return to the White House, but only one, Grover Cleveland, was successful. Martin Van Buren, Millard Fillmore, and Theodore Roosevelt all tried to use third party movements to recapture the White House but failed. John Tyler, the first vice-president to become president upon the death of a president, wanted to return to the presidency, but finally settled for a seat in the Confederate Congress.

Nearly every president has been critical of his successor. Even George Washington criticized John Adams for spending too much time away from his office. Some former presidents have served in advisory roles after leaving the White House. Grover Cleveland headed a commission to resolve a coal strike in 1902, Taft was cochairman of the War Labor Board during World War I, and Herbert Hoover served as the director of famine relief following World War II and later as head of a commission to study the executive branch of government.

Before 1958, presidents had to rely on their own financial resources, and the result was often disastrous. Thomas Jefferson retired to his plantation at Monticello but slowly fell heavily in debt and died broke. There were sporadic suggestions that former presidents should receive some type of pension, and Congress did appropriate money to help the destitute widows of some presidents.

In the past two decades, the position of former president has become almost an unofficial office. Former presidents are provided with staffs, Secret Service protection, allowances, and a pension, and they receive briefings on current issues from White House aides.

Even with the benefits, four recent former presidents, Jimmy Carter, Gerald Ford, Richard Nixon, and Lyndon Johnson wanted to remain in power; their departure was bitter, and the loss of power and prestige dramatic.

This book tells the stories of the men who served as president and how they spent their lives after leaving the White House.

Acknowledgments

Many people have given their time to assist in the preparation of this book.

Researchers in both the photographic section and the manuscript collection of the Library of Congress provided great amounts of help and guidance.

As always, my editors at *The Orlando Sentinel,* Bill Dunn, David Burgin and *Sentinel* publisher, Harold Lifvendahl, have been unfailingly supportive and helpful.

Editors at *The Washington Post* provided access to the paper's files.

As he has many times, James Donna of The Associated Press came to my rescue.

Dotty Breitbart, the editor for this book, was patient in guiding me through the publishing process, and for all of her assistance I am grateful.

And finally, to my wife Jane, who read the manuscript and offered scores of helpful suggestions, my love and affection.

J.C.C.

Contents

George Washington

—— **one** ——

The world had never seen a government like the democracy practiced in the United States. The leader of a nation did not give up power: he might die or be overthrown, but no one walked away from power. The men who wrote the Constitution set no limits on a president's length of service, and many assumed that George Washington would serve until he died. Washington, however, said that in order for democracy to survive, power must be passed on from one president to another.

He had wanted to leave office after a single term, going as far as to draft a farewell speech, but the pressures and pleas of friends pushed him to serve a second term. "I would rather be in my grave than in the presidency," he said. But he would not remain after his second term, establishing a two-term tradition, which would last for nearly a century and a half.

Although it is probable that he hoped his vice-president and fellow Federalist, John Adams, would become president, Washington showed no interest in the campaign. He clearly looked forward to retirement, writing to his step-grandson, "As the curtain of my political life is about to drop, I am, as you may suppose, a great deal hurried in the closing scenes of it."

To General Henry Knox, his one-time comrade in arms, he wrote, "To the wearied traveler who sees a resting place and is bending his body to lean thereon, I now compare myself, but to be suffered to do this in peace is, I perceive, too much to be endured by some. . . . Although the prospect of retirement is most grateful

1

to my soul, and I have not a wish to mix again in the great world or to partake in its politics, yet I am not without regret at parting with (perhaps never more to meet) the few intimates whom I love."

Adams won the election, and on March 4, 1797, the peaceful transition from one leader to another took place. But even in Adams's finest hour, Washington occupied center stage. Adams arrived for the inauguration in a pearl-colored suit with a sword and cockade. Washington wore a simple black coat, but the tears in the crowd were for Washington. Adams complained that Washington seemed "to enjoy a triumph over me. Methought I heard him say, 'Aye! I'm fairly out and you fairly in. See which of us will be happiest!'"

His eight years as president had proven to be expensive for while Congress appropriated some money for furnishing his Philadelphia residence, he was forced to buy much of his furniture. To keep up the standard he thought the president should have, he was forced to sell thousands of acres of his Western land.

Because Washington had purchased much of his own furniture for the executive mansion, he decided to offer it to Adams—for a price. He put a price on each item, the chandelier with 8 lights for $300, the chain on which it hung would cost an additional $10, and the list ran on. Adams considered the offer, but in the end rejected it.

The move to Mount Vernon was complicated by the large number of possessions Washington had accumulated. An invoice showed that he had shipped 97 boxes, 14 trunks, 43 casks, 1 ton of iron, 4 bundles of rod nails, 1 toilet table, 1 tin shower bath and hundreds of other items. He complained that the move was almost too much. "On one side, I am called upon to remember the parrot; on the other, to remember the dog. For my own part, I should not pine if both were forgot."

He promised himself that once back at Mount Vernon, he would not travel again more than 20 miles from home and looked forward to "more real enjoyment than in all the business with which I have been occupied for upwards of forty years." The return to Mount Vernon was marked by large crowds.

He found Mount Vernon in serious neglect and in need of extensive repairs. He hired dozens of workmen to do the work. "I am already surrounded by joiners, masons, painters, etc., . . . I have scarcely a room to put a friend into or to sit in myself without the music of hammers, or the odoriferous smell of paint," he said. Soon he began to complain about the pace and quality of their work. "Workmen in most countries, I believe, are necessary plagues. In this, where entreaties as well as money must be used to obtain their work and keep them to their duty, they baffle all calculations."

Once back at Mount Vernon he fell into a routine, rising at dawn, eating breakfast and then, "I mount my horse and ride round my farms, which employs me until it is time to dress for dinner, at which I rarely miss seeing strange faces, come, as they say, out of respect to me. . . . Having given you the history of a day, it will serve for a year."

In an effort to reduce his involvement in politics, he stopped reading daily newspapers. "For myself, having turned aside from the broad walks of political, into the narrow paths of private life, I shall leave it with those, whose duty it is to consider subjects of this sort, and (as every good citizen ought to do) conform to whatsoever the ruling powers shall decide."

He was sixty-five, and except for frequent colds, his health was good. He worked hard, supervising his vast plantation and hundreds of slaves. By any standard, he was the country's most famous citizen, and his fame brought many visitors to Mount Vernon, some complete strangers, who came to meet him. He often protested about the many visitors but clearly loved the attention and the contact it provided with the outside world. He once called his home "a well regulated tavern."

Like many large plantation owners, Washington suffered serious cash flow problems. The combination of his presidential salary and money from his farms had enabled him to meet expenses during his presidency, but without the salary he was strapped. Each year he was forced to sell off some of his Western land. In September 1799, he wrote, "were it not for occasional supplies of money in payment for lands sold within the last four or five years in the amount of upwards of $50,000," Washington said he would be "in debt and difficulties."

He was still a wealthy man, despite his frequent cash shortages. He had been buying land for nearly half a century, and it had increased dramatically in value. In making his will, he placed his worth at $488,137, including $25,212 in stocks and 34,000 acres. "My estate, though it might sell on credit for a tolerable sum, has been and probably will continue to be an unproductive one."

Land speculation had come into vogue, just as playing the stock market would become a national past time more than a century later. Washington saw a chance to make a large profit by selling his land to speculators, who in turn would subdivide it and sell it to immigrants. He started pushing his land, extolling its virtues to anyone who would listen. The problem with the whole scheme was that few speculators had the cash to buy the land outright, so financing was required. Far too many speculators did not have the resources to meet the payments: they hoped to buy the land, sell it quickly, and realize a profit.

Washington said he received more than his share of "the vague, speculative, and unmeaning offers of men who have no wherewithall to fill an engagement and do not mean (more than probable) to do it."

Washington, despite his misgivings, fell in with one such speculator. He sold thousands of acres of his Pennsylvania land to James Welch, a man with a shady reputation. Welch was not even able to make the first payment and Washington wrote him:

> I am in extreme want of money which you gave a solemn promise I should receive the first of January last. . . . however you may have succeeded in imposing upon others you shall not practice the like game with me with impunity. . . . It would be uncandid, Mr. Welch, not to inform you that I have heard too much of your character lately not to expect talk after talk, and relation after relation of your numerous disappointments by way of excuses for the noncompliance of your agreement with me; but this, I assure you, will not answer your purposes.

When Welch still did not make a payment, Washington took back the land and never again sold it.

To other debtors, Washington would threaten lawsuits and send dunning letters. He often told his debtors that he desperately needed the money, painting a picture of impending bankruptcy if the payment was not forthcoming. In 1799, for the first time in his life, Washington was forced to borrow money. He received a $1,500 loan from the Bank of Alexandria. He despised the idea of "a necessity of borrowing from the banks at ruinous interest."

An outgoing president turns over more than the presidency to his successor: he turns over the problems of his administration. No new president gets an entirely clean slate: the woes of his predecessor come with the job. During the Washington administration, relations with the French government had become strained. France and Britain had gone to war during Washington's administration and Washington had favored the British.

Under the Adams administration things went from bad to worse, and it appeared that war with France was imminent. Adams pushed through legislation to authorize an army of 10,000 men and a provisional army of 50,000 more men. The nation was deeply divided over the possibility of war, and Adams realized that he would need to mobilize popular support. He wrote to Washington asking him to once again serve his country. "I must tax you sometimes for advice. We must have your name if you will, in any case, permit us to use it." Adams wanted Washington to return to uniform, to lead the U.S. armies.

Washington replied, "In the case of an actual invasion by a formidable force, I certainly should not entrench myself under the cover of age and retirement." Adams nominated Washington to be lieutenant general and commander of all military forces and Congress gave its quick and unanimous approval.

Although Washington had said he was willing to help, he had no idea that Adams planned to name him commander of the armies so quickly. He learned of his appointment from the newspapers. Adams wrote to Washington apologizing for acting without informing him. "If it had been in my power to nominate you President of the United States, I should have done it with less hesitation and more pleasure." He said he owed Washington "all the apologies I can make."

Washington accepted the commission saying, "I shall relinquish the peaceful walk to which I have retired, and in the shades of which I had fondly hoped to spend the remnants of a life, worn down with cares." The post paid $250 a month.

Although he accepted the appointment, Washington had serious reservations about the course being followed by the Adams administration and about the abilities of Adams. Early on he had said that Adams was spending too much time at his Massachusetts home and losing popular support. In 1798, he wrote, "I have for some time past, viewed the political concerns of the United States with an anxious eye. They appear to me to be moving by hasty strides to some awful crisis. . . ."

On November 5, 1798, Washington accompanied by an aide and four servants set out for Philadelphia where he spent five weeks making arrangements for his new army. He clearly enjoyed the return to the social life of Philadelphia, purchasing a fancy dress uniform to wear and attending many dinners with old friends. For one friend, conditions had changed dramatically. Robert Morris, the man who helped finance the Revolutionary War, had lost everything in land speculation and ended in debtors' prison. But Washington had not forgotten Morris and his invaluable help and one night went to the prison to have dinner with Morris.

While Washington worked to organize an army, the threat of war gradually began to recede. The French showed a new willingness to compromise and Washington urged Adams to use any means to avoid war. By 1799 it was clear that Adams was in deep political trouble and the Federalists feared that he would lose the election of 1800 to their archenemy, Thomas Jefferson.

Governor John Trumbull of Connecticut wrote to Washington in July 1799 suggesting that he consider running for president again. Washington said no:

> It would be criminal therefore in me, although it should be the wish of my countrymen and I could be elected, to accept an office under this conviction, which another would discharge with more ability. . . . I should be charged not only with irresolution, but with concealed ambition which waits only an occasion to blaze out; and, in short, with dotage and imbecility.

Washington returned to Mount Vernon and plunged into farming, working out a complicated plan to rotate his crops. The soil at Mount Vernon had long ago worn thin, making it difficult to grow crops. Washington detailed the use for every acre, beginning in 1800 and continuing through 1803. The final document ran between 30,000 and 40,000 words. He finished the paper in 1799, but did not live long enough to see it put into action.

On December 12, 1799, Washington went riding in a snow storm and when he returned to his mansion, his secretary, Tobias Lear noted, "I observed to him that I was afraid he had got wet. He said, no; his greatcoat had kept him dry—but his neck appeared wet and the snow was hanging on his hair. . . . He came to dinner without changing his dress. In the evening, he appeared as well as usual."

The following day, Washington complained of a sore throat, but refused to take medication. "You know I never take anything for a cold. Let it go as it came," he said.

In the early morning of December 14, he awoke his wife and said he was having trouble breathing. In the morning, an overseer who usually treated the medical problems of the slaves was sent for. Washington demanded that the overseer bleed him and the overseer cut Washngton's arm and let the blood flow. Two doctors were sent for, both of whom bled Washington even more. He was unable to swallow, and whenever he tried, he nearly choked to death.

The two doctors disagreed about the treatment. Unable to agree, he decided to bleed Washington for a fourth time as his strength slowly ebbed away. Washington turned to one of the doctors and said, "Doctor, I die hard, but I am not afraid to go. . . . My breath cannot last long."

He rested briefly, then said to his doctors, "I feel myself going, I thank you for your attention. You had better not take any more trouble about me; but let me go off quietly; I cannot last long."

Day turned to night and it was clear the end was near. Washington was having difficulty speaking and needed all of his strength to say, "I am just going. Have me decently buried, and do not let my body be put into the vault in less than three days after I am dead."

He said to the doctor, "Do you understand me?"

"Yes sir," one of the doctors replied.

"Tis well," Washington said.

About midnight, he died.

John Adams

On November 1, 1800, John Adams, the second president of the United States moved into the still unfinished Executive Mansion in Washington, D.C. His stay would be short; within days, he was defeated by Thomas Jefferson, becoming the first president to be turned out of office. On March 4, 1801, Adams left Washington as soon as his term ended, not even attending Jefferson's inauguration.

For Adams, life had been bittersweet; throughout his life, his accomplishments had been overshadowed by others. As a revolutionary leader in Boston, he played a second role to Samuel Adams; as one of the authors of the Declaration of Independence he found the major credit going to Jefferson, and he was vice-president when George Washington was selected president. Now, he was going home to Massachusetts after being rejected by the voters. He was an old sixty-five years, tired after more than a quarter century of tireless government service.

Before leaving Washington, he rejected an idea from his supporters to name himself to the Supreme Court saying that while the offer was very flattering, he was too old and had "neglected the study of law for six and twenty years." He left with a feeling of bitterness, writing to a friend, "Clouds black and gloomy hang over our country," and to another friend he wrote, "We shall be tossed in the tempestuous sea of liberty for years to come."

He returned to his home in Quincy and for months brooded about his defeat, trying to figure out why the voters had turned against him. In the end, he decided that his actions had been correct. It was the voters who did not understand; they had been wrong. Until he died, he would constantly turn over in his mind the events that led to his defeat, explaining to anyone who cared to listen exactly what had brought on his defeat.

In 1815, he wrote to a friend listing his accomplishments, but added, "For all this I was turned out of office, degraded and disgraced by my country;　and I was glad of it. I felt no disgrace because I felt no remorse."

He settled into his family home, a large country house which seemed to sprawl with additions in every direction to suit the needs of a man with a very large family of children, grandchildren, nephews, nieces, and relatives suffering from financial distress.

He quickly adapted to the quiet life, working hard at various chores around the house. He was up at dawn, put on his work clothes and then tackled whatever task was at hand. Gradually, the hard work outdoors improved his health. His son, John Quincy Adams, thought it would help his father to write an autobiography. At first Adams rejected the idea, which he said would "engage my feelings and inflame my passions. . . . It would set me on fire and I should have occasion for a bucket of water constantly by my side to put it out." But John Quincy Adams did not give up and in 1804 finally convinced his father to start writing.

He yearned to return to his law practice but dismissed it as impossible. "My greatest grief is that I cannot return to the bar. There I should forget in a moment that I was ever a member of Congress, a foreign minister or President of the United States. But I cannot speak," a reference to a vocal cord ailment.

He began to devote more time to reading, writing to a friend, "I want to learn the Chinese language and to study all the Asiatic researches." He stayed away from political books, but he continued to be interested in politics. Although the country was just sixteen years old, he thought he saw a pattern which would influence future presidential elections. He said one political group would rule for about a dozen years, then another on the opposite side of the political spectrum would take control. "Our government will be a game of leapfrog of factions, leaping over one another's back about once in twelve years according to my computation." In the defeat of the Federalists he saw that pattern. "When a party grows strong and feels its power, it becomes intoxicated, grows presumptuous and extravagant and breaks to pieces."

In addition to his reading, Adams dramatically increased his correspondence, writing to friends on almost any subject. On banking: "The banking infatuation pervades all America. Our whole system of banks is a violation of every honest principle of banks. There is no honest bank but a bank of deposit. A bank that issues paper at interest is a pickpocket or a robber."

He became an opponent of Jefferson's administration, viewing it as democracy run amok. He wrote of the "strange, awkward, and outlandish vagabonds running about in every town in the character of lay preachers, schoolmasters, peddlers, day laborers and beggars watching every opportunity to preach democracy. . . ."

He criticized Jefferson for what he saw as a lack of leadership and poor policy. "Our country is in masquerade! No party, no man dares to avow his real sentiments. All is disguise, vizard, cloak. The people are totally puzzled and confounded. . . . If I was only forty years old, I would as I did at that age set all disguise and fear at defiance, and once more lead my country."

Already, there was talk of disunion and it worried Adams, who wrote, "Mingled rage and fear (are) now the predominant passions in our nation." To another friend he wrote, "Americans, I fondly hope and candidly believe, are not yet arrived at the age of Demosthenes or Cicero. If we can preserve our Union entire we may preserve our Republic. But if the Union is broken we become two petty principalities, little better than our feudatories, one of France and the other of England."

He blamed the nation's problems on Jefferson, who was completing his second term. "He must know that he leaves the country infinitely worse than he found it, and that from his own error or ignorance." He said Jefferson "has honored and salaried almost every villan he could find who had been an enemy to me."

Adams lived frugally, and although he had never been wealthy, he had managed to save his money. He suffered a major financial setback when a London firm failed and took with it $10,000 that Adams had invested. Fortunately, his wife Abigail was able to run the large household with economy. The farm provided some food but little money, and their income came principally from securities Abigail had purchased over the years.

After Jefferson left the White House, Adams's attitude began to mellow toward the man who had defeated him. Through a mutual friend, Dr. Benjamin Rush, the two once more began ex-changing letters, more than 200 between 1811 and 1826.

Adams divided his time between his farm, his reading, and ac-tivity in a number of organizations. He was president of the Amer-ican Academy of Arts and Sciences, a member of the Mas-sachusetts Society for Promoting Agriculture, and a member of the Board of Visitors at Harvard University. His memberships meant frequent trips to Boston where he met with old friends who shared his political views.

In 1812, the United States went to war with England, and Adams felt that he had been vindicated. He thought his adminis-tration was working to insure peace, and that the Jefferson Admin-istration made war inevitable.

Adams had five children; a daughter Susanna died in infancy. The other four included a daughter, nicknamed Nabby, and sons Charles, Boylston, and John Quincy. Charles died shortly before the end of Adams's presidency, the result of too much liquor; Boylston became a successful lawyer, and John Quincy attained the greatest fame, rising to the presidency.

As the years passed, death became a common occurrence for Adams; an infant granddaughter died in the same room where Adams had been born. In grief, he cried out, "Why was I preserved three quarters of a century, and that rose cropped in the bud?" His daughter, Nabby, returned home to die, suffering from terminal cancer. In the room next to Nabby was Sally Adams, the widow of Charles, who was suffering from consumption.

Three weeks after she returned home, Nabby died and Adams wrote to Jefferson, "I can proceed no further with this letter. Your friend, my only daughter, expired yesterday in the forty-ninth year of her age . . . forty-six of which she was the healthiest and firmest of us all; since which she had been a monument to suffering and patience."

His old friend, Elbridge Gerry, died in 1814 and he wrote, "I am left alone . . . not one of my contemporaries and colleagues is left."

In 1818, Abigail suffered a stroke shortly after the couple cele-brated their fifty-fourth wedding anniversary. She could neither move nor speak, and it was clear that death was near. On the tenth of November, she died with her husband by her side. "The bitter-ness of death is past," he wrote, "the grim spoiler so terrible to human nature has no sting left for me." For Adams himself, health was becoming a worry. He wrote only with great pain and was forced to dictate his letters. He could not get over the loss of Abigail and was often deeply depressed. He wrote to a friend, "My house is a region of sorrow. . . . Never in my whole life was I more perplexed or distressed than at this moment." In another letter he said, "The world falls to pieces round me, my friends and my enemies disappear."

To his son, John Quincy, he wrote about "the comfortable prospect of dying peaceably in my own bed, surrounded by amiable and affectionate children, kind neighbors, and excellent friends."

As the years passed, Adams believed that the fate of the nation was secure. To add to his pride was the selection of John Quincy Adams to be secretary of state under James Monroe.

Still, his thoughts turned increasingly to death. To a friend, he wrote, "I am not tormented with the fear of death; now through suffering under many infirmities and agitated by many afflictions, weary of life. . . . We shall leave the world with many consolations; it is better than we found it—superstition, persecution, and bigotry are somewhat abated, governments are a little ameliorated, science and literature are greatly improved and more widely spread. Our country has brilliant and exhilarating prospects before us."

Adams still had one more role to play. In 1779, at the age of forty-four, he had almost single handedly written the Massachusetts state constitution. In 1820, at the age of eighty-five, Adams was called back by the citizens of Quincy as their representative to the convention to draft a new state constitution. Adams, who thought that he had largely been forgotten, was overjoyed, moving to Boston for the sessions at the State House. He contributed little to the drafting of the document, although his old fire returned when the subject of voting rights came up. At issue was whether the right to vote would be extended to those who did not own property.

Adams spoke out strongly for the property qualification. He pointed to the horror of the French Revolution and said that those who owned property would merely buy the votes of those who were too poor to purchase property. But the times had changed, democracy had progressed, and Adams was almost alone when the vote came.

The activity of the convention took its toll on Adams, leaving him with a fever and forcing him to spend two months in bed. He recovered slightly, but wrote to a friend comparing his health with an old watch, "Its spring and wheels so completely worn out that it can clip no longer. The hour, minute, and second hands all useless."

Just as the Massachusetts convention had given Adams something to look forward to in 1820, the events of 1822 gave him a new reason to fight for life. There was growing talk that his son, John Quincy, would be a candidate for president in 1824. The campaign was rugged; Adams was pitted against the popular Andrew Jackson and two regional favorites, Henry Clay and W.H. Crawford. The opponents of John Quincy brought up old charges against his father as the campaign grew increasingly bitter. In November, Jackson easily won the popular vote and led in the electoral college, but he could not claim a majority of electoral votes. The contest was thrown in the House of Representatives where, after a great deal of maneuvering, Adams emerged the winner. John Adams wept when he heard the news.

In 1826, the nation was celebrating the fiftieth anniversary of the signing of the Declaration of Independence, but Adams was far too sick to join in any of the celebrations. He was dying and as the Fourth of July approached, his friends and family gathered to be near the ninety-year-old Adams. On the morning of the fourth, he fell into a coma but around noon rallied briefly and with great effort said just three words, "Thomas Jefferson survives." He sank back into the coma, regained consciousness once again, tried to speak but could not. At six o'clock he died.

Ironically, his final words were incorrect. At Monticello, Thomas Jefferson had died a few hours earlier.

Thomas Jefferson

three

After eight years as president, Thomas Jefferson's administration came to an end on March 4, 1809. Eight state legislatures had passed resolutions urging him to seek a third term, but Jefferson replied, "The weight of public business begins to be too heavy for me, and I long for the enjoyment of rural life. . . . After all I am entitled to my discharge." To others he said, "Never did a prisoner, released from chains, feel such relief as I shall on shaking off the shackles of power. . . ." On Inauguration Day, Jefferson was not ready to leave the White House, so the incoming president, James Madison, told him to remain until he was packed. Jefferson stayed an additional week.

He was leaving Washington with his finances in disarray. Jefferson was forced to borrow money to cover the debts he had incurred while president; the total was $11,000. His papers were loaded onto two wagons, and his plants were placed in a third wagon for the trip to Monticello.

He was sixty-six years old, and the scars of a lifetime of government service showed, but his retirement was to be troubled by the financial problems that would haunt him for the remainder of his life. He estimated his worth at $225,000 including more than 10,000 acres of land, 200 slaves, and a manufacturing mill. His holdings included the beautiful Natural Bridge. But the figures were terribly misleading; his assets consisted only of land and slaves, which were not particularly profitable. Only a third of Jefferson's slaves actually worked in the field; the rest were house slaves or artisans.

His income could not pay his expenses, and each year until he died, he sunk deeper into debt. He owed money to British firms from loans made before the Revolutionary War and money to a Dutch financial institution for a loan made in the 1790s. He paid old debts by borrowing new money, and with the additional interest there was no way he would ever move into the black. Nearly every year, he drafted a plan to pay off his debts, but he usually overestimated his income and underestimated his debts. He owned a nail-making business but fell behind in his payments to the firm that supplied his materials and was forced to ask for a delay in making his payments.

In his first year of retirement, he was unable to renew an $8,000 debt, and shifted it to the Bank of Virginia. But in the seventeen years that remained in his life, he would never be able to pay the debt completely. To pay his debts, he began selling his land, starting with 474 acres in Bedford. The Scottish firm of Henderson, McCaul & Company finally pressed its long overdue debt, writing Jefferson that its American representative was "in distress for money." The money owed to the firm is a dramatic example of Jefferson's plight. It had started out in 1775 as a $250 debt to a merchant which was assigned to Henderson, McCaul & Company. In 1811, Jefferson made a $1,000 payment, but the interest had accumulated to such an extent that the debt was not entirely paid.

When the British burned the Library of Congress during the War of 1812, Jefferson agreed to sell his personal library to the government. The 10,000 volumes had cost him $50,000; in his desperation he agreed to sell them for $23,500, but still the money repaid only half of his debts. No sooner had the sale been completed than a drought nearly destroyed his crops. In the spring of 1817, he wrote that his animals were nearly starving to death because of the lack of forage.

In 1812, as the threat of war with Britain loomed, President James Madison asked Jefferson to serve as secretary of state. Jefferson, now sixty-eight, said he was too old and that his mind had become "so dissolved in tranquility" that it could "never again encounter a contentious assembly."

In retirement, he was able to mend his long-standing rift with John Adams. He and Adams began exchanging letters in 1814. Obviously concerned about his health, Jefferson wrote, "Our machines have been running now seventy or eighty years, and we must expect that, worn as they are, here a pictor, there a wheel, now a pinion, next a spring, will be giving away; and, however we may tinker up for a while, all will at length cease motion."

His correspondence consumed a large amount of his time. He computed that he wrote an average of 1,267 letters a year and asked a friend, "Is this life? At best it is but the life of a millhorse, who sees no end to his circle but in death. To such a life, that of a cabbage is paradise."

In 1821, he began writing his autobiography, jotting down the opening sentence, "At the age of 77, I begin to make some memoranda, and state some recollections of dates and facts concerning myself, for my own ready reference, and for the information of my family." He wrote nearly 40,000 words, then stopped.

The years went by, and the debts continued to mount. In 1817, the Dutch firm pressed him for the $6,000 he owed. Again, as with the Scottish debt, this one had been made years before, starting out as a $2,000 loan, but gaining interest. He stepped up the pace of his round-robin borrowing, making loans at one bank to pay off another. A further setback came in 1817 when his wheat crop failed. Jefferson borrowed from the Bank of the United States, where the president was Wilson Cary Nicholas, a friend and distant relative. Unfortunately, the loan by Nicholas obligated Jefferson to the financier, and he agreed to cosign two $10,000 notes for Nicholas, and later cosigned additional notes. Unfortunately, Nicholas's position was as shaky as Jefferson's.

The former president was borrowing from anybody with money. When he made a trip to help select as site for what would become the University of Virginia, he had to borrow $100 from a merchant to finance the journey.

Like the losing bettor who eventually blames the bookie, Jefferson became bitter against the banks. It was the banks which led him down the path of easy loans and into suffocating debts. He wrote to a friend, "The enormous abuses of the banking system are not only prostrating our commerce, but producing a resolution of property."

His plight worsened in 1819. The price of flour was falling, making his mills financial drains, and the banks were tightening up their loans. He decided to sell some land, but found that land prices had been forced down by a growing economic panic. He wrote, "To owe what I cannot pay is a constant torment."

Nicholas, whose own financial empire was about to crumble asked Jefferson to cosign two additional $10,000 notes, which Jefferson readily did. Just when it seemed that things could not become worse for Jefferson, they did. Nicholas went under, forced to turn his property over to trustees. He wrote to Jefferson saying he believed his assets could pay off his debts and that Jefferson would not be called upon to make good the $40,000 in notes he had cosigned for Nicholas.

Jefferson wrote, "Never were such hard times seen as we have here now. Not a dollar is passing from one to another." The mill was producing no money and his list of creditors continued to grow. He sold more land, but the money could do little more than meet his most pressing bills.

By the standards of the early nineteenth century, Jefferson was a very old man, but his health remained generally good until 1825, when he was eighty-three. His physician outlined Jefferson's condition in a memo to him. He was suffering from an inflammation of the urinary canal caused by problems with his prostrate gland.

He played almost no role in politics in his final years, but was the leader in efforts to found what is now the University of Virginia. Beginning in 1816, Jefferson played the key role in the school's establishment, fighting against opponents and lobbying for support in the general assembly, where it survived its first committee vote by the barest of margins. Finally the House of Delegates agreed to the establishment of the school (originally to be called Central College). But the legislature appropriated just $15,000 a year to operate the college, far less than necessary. He served on the committee which chose Charlottesville as a site, designed the buildings, helped choose the faculty and he served as the first rector.

As with any new college, there were problems. He had trouble recruiting a faculty although he was pleased with the men he was able to attract. But it was the student body that troubled him the most. He said the students could be divided into thirds: one third were reasonably diligent, one third hard working and ambitious, and the other third were dismissed as "idle rambles incapable of application."

His home was a gathering place for students, who frequently came for Sunday dinner. Rules at the university were rarely en-

forced, class rolls seldom taken, and generally the professors enforced the rules they wanted to enforce. The students took advan-
tage of the situation, bringing liquor onto the campus; a student
threw a bottle through the window of a professor, and, finally, a
group of masked students created a disturbance.

Two professors attempting to investigate the disturbance received insults, and a stone was thrown at one of the men. The
breakdown of order concerned Jefferson and the other members of
the Board of Visitors, who finally revised the rules to ensure en-
forcement. The trips to the University adversely affected Jefferson's health: his hearing was nearly gone, his memory frequently
failed, and the pains in his body became more difficult to deal with.

It was the University of Virginia which took him away, if only
temporarily, from his financial and health problems. He worried
about the smallest detail, supervising the purchase of additional
land and construction of the Rotunda to house the university library.

As the years passed, he gradually became responsible for
more and more of the debts of his relatives. The new burden, in addition to the debts of his own making, forced him to realize that no
matter how many plans he came up with to eliminate the debts,
they would not work.

Beginning in January of 1826, Jefferson hatched a new plan, a
national lottery to bail him out of his financial distress. Since he was
unable to sell his land for anything approaching a fair market
value, he would sell lottery tickets with the winner receiving a por-
tion of his property. For Jefferson, it was a desperate move; he had
long been an opponent of gambling and speculation, but now he
desperately needed the money. A lottery was not an uncommon
method for raising money, but usually it was used by charities and
public causes. Jefferson was both a charity and a public cause, but
he needed permission of the legislature to hold his lottery.

To get that permission, Jefferson began lobbying, telling
friends that without the lottery, he would have to sell Monticello.
The lobbying was unnecessary; there was no way the legislature
could turn down Jefferson.

He had hoped that the lottery would give him enough money
to save Monticello, but now he realized that to pay all of his bills
and get enough to live one, his beloved home would have to be included in the lottery. The news of Jefferson's financial difficulties

spread throughout the nation, bringing forth an outpouring of sympathy and offers of help. From the outpouring came a new scheme. Tickets would be purchased; the money turned over to Jefferson; but then the tickets would be burned on July 4, 1826, the fiftieth anniversary of the signing of the Declaration of Independence. Under the plan, 11,480 tickets would be sold at ten dollars apiece. His appeal raised nearly $16,000 and moved Jefferson to say, "I have spent three times as much money, and given my whole life to my countrymen, and now they nobly come forward in the only way they can, to repay me and save an old servant from being turned like a dog out of doors. . . . Not a cent of this is wrung from the taxpayer; it is the pure unsolicited offering of love."

But the money was coming too late; Jefferson's health was rapidly declining. In late June, it was clear that Jefferson could not last. He remained coherent, but his doctors had given up all hope. On July 4, 1826, the day he had hoped his financial worries would end, he died at 12:50 P.M.

Before he died, he had written the words he wanted placed on his tombstone. "Here lies buried Thomas Jefferson, author of the Declaration of American Independence, of the statute of Virginia for religious freedom, and father of the University of Virginia." He did not mention that he had served as president of the United States.

James Madison

—— four ——

James Madison, the last of the Founding Fathers to serve as president, remained in Washington for a month following the inauguration of his successor, James Monroe. It was a month of parties and dinners, but when Madison finally left on April 6, it was for the last time. He retired to his 5,000 acre estate in Virginia, intent on living the life of a gentleman planter. At the age of sixty-six, Madison had given his life to serving his state and country.

But he could not completely escape public service. He agreed to serve with his friend and mentor, Thomas Jefferson, on the Board of Visitors to help plan for what would become the University of Virginia. He was elected president of the local agricultural society and published his views on farming, which proved to be years ahead of their time. He called for crop rotation, the limitation of timber cutting, reforestation, and improved breeding of livestock.

And Madison, a slaveholder, found himself drawn into the rising debate over slavery. He wrote to Robert J. Evans, the Philadelphia abolitionist, that slaves should be freed gradually, with concern for the right of the slaveholder. He did not believe slaves could remain in the United States once they were freed and put forward a plan to purchase freedom for the slaves. By selling 300 million acres of government-owned lands at two dollars an acre, the government would be able to buy the one and a half million slaves and send them back to Africa. In 1825, he endorsed a plan to purchase land in Tennessee for freed slaves, but the plan did not materialize.

He received a letter from Jefferson welcoming him back to Virginia. "I sincerely congratulate you on your release from incessant labors, corroding anxieties, active enemies & interested friends, & on your return to your books & farm, to tranquility & independence. A day of these is worth ages of the former."

As other presidents had discovered, a lifetime of public service may bring fame and prestige, but the financial rewards are small. His charitable attitude toward his slaves had left him with a disproportionate number of older slaves who could not work, but still had to be fed, clothed, and housed. The Madison plantation supported 100 slaves when times were good, but a series of rainless summers destroyed the crops. There were other unforeseen financial difficulties. A turnpike company Madison had invested in went bankrupt, leaving him responsible for nearly $2,000 in debts.

The irresponsible behavior of Madison's stepson added to his financial plight. Payne Todd had run up large bills without any means of repaying them. Eventually, the bills came to Madison, who tried valiantly to pay them. A Washington lottery house demanded $500 which Madison paid immediately, but he had to plead with a Philadelphia landlord for more time to pay a bill and not throw this stepson in prison. Todd wrote a number of bad checks, which Madison helped to make good, while his friends paid others. Despite his best efforts, Todd frequently went to debtors prison, but each time Madison raised the necessary money to bail him out. When Madison died, his records showed that he had paid $20,000 of Todd's bills. Madison's wife Dolley, already upset about her son's failure to settle down, was never told about the payments until after Madison's death.

By 1833, the poor national economy dealt Madison another blow. He was forced to sell three of his farms, but he refused to sell the slaves that worked the farms. They were brought back to his plantation, which contributed to the overpopulation. His debts continued to grow and the following year he was forced to sell 16 slaves for $6,000, but it was still not enough to pay his bills. Madison applied to the Bank of The United States for a loan to cover his debts. However, his credit was so poor he was turned down.

Madison blamed the poor Southern economy on slavery. To a friend he wrote that he planned to free his slaves upon his death. He said that dramatic increases in the slave population were contributing to the decline of the South. In 1833, he became president of the American Colonization Society, which had begun resettling slaves in Liberia. He seemed to sense the trouble that was to come, asking if the elimination of slavery was not "preferable to a torpid acquiescence in a perpetuation of slavery, or an extinguishment of it by convulsions more disasterous in their character and consequences than slavery itself?" And he had nothing but scorn for the "idea of the Southern States being able to maintain a rising against the North." He told a visitor that any nation that had a servile population would be in conflict with those who were totally free.

When he surrendered the presidency to Monroe, Madison decided not to become involved in politics again, but in 1829 his state called him back to serve as a member of a convention drafting a new Virginia constitution. Drafting the document to create the United States had proven to be an almost impossible task but bringing together the political and economic factions in Virginia would be even more difficult.

In the Eastern part of the state there were large landowners, accustomed to controlling the state. But the Western residents were small farmers with few slaves, and they wanted the state to spend money to make improvements in transportation. Under the Virginia Constitution, slaves had no rights but were counted in the census. That gave the slaveowners control of the legislature and embittered the Westerners.

For Madison, it would be an attempt to turn back the clock more than four decades to when he had played a pivotal role in drafting the U.S. Constitution. The trip to Richmond was the first time Madison had left his home in a dozen years, but it was all in vain. The magic of the Philadelphia convention could not be repeated. As he had done in Philadelphia, Madison proposed that slaves be counted as three-fifths of a person, a compromise which would have left the Eastern slaveholders in firm control of the legislature, but given the Westerners greater representation. Even so, the Eastern forces saw no reason to compromise. Madison had envisioned a constitution that would last for a century, but the document produced in Richmond was so poor that it survived just 31 years.

By 1831, Madison's health had declined dramatically. He was bedridden with rheumatism, and in May 1832 he wrote, "I am still confined to my bed, with my malady, my debility and my age, in tripple alliance against me."

The seeds of the Civil War were planted by South Carolina in 1832 when it passed an ordinance forbidding the federal government to collect duties within the state. The state threatened to leave the Union if any attempt was made to collect the duties by force. Madison became a central figure because he was the last surviving member of the Founding Fathers and could offer the best account of what they had intended in drafting the Constitution. The supporters of South Carolina's position argued that the intent of Madison and his fellow authors had been to give the right of nullification to the states, but Madison would have none of it. He strongly supported Andrew Jackson's stand against nullification and helped keep Virginia from joining South Carolina. He called nullification and secession "twin heresies" and said they "ought to be buried in the same grave."

The crisis passed, but Madison saw clearly that greater dangers lay ahead. He wrote to Henry Clay that South Carolina's action had left "the torch of discord." The Civil War was 28 years in the future, but Madison said that South Carolina had suggested disunion and had opened up a possibility that would create further troubles.

In 1832, Madison drew up his will, leaving all of his property to his wife except for some minor bequests to friends and relatives. But he went back on his word to free his slaves upon his death. With his other property, they would go to his wife.

Now past eighty, Madison's condition continued to decline. On June 27, 1836, he was unable to swallow his breakfast and his niece said, "What is the matter, Uncle James?"

He replied, "Nothing more than a change of mind, my dear." With that his head dropped, and he died.

He left behind $21,000 in debts and his original notes on the drafting of the Constitution. He thought his wife Dolly would be able to sell his notes to a publisher and profit handsomely, but she was unable to sell them. Finally, Congress came to his widow's rescue, purchasing his notes on the Constitutional Convention for $30,000. Dolly moved to Washington and put her irresponsible son, Payne Todd, in charge of Madison's estate, Montpelier. His mismanagement forced Dolly to sell the estate for far less than its true value and once again, Congress came to her aid, this time buying Madison's correspondence. She spent the rest of her life in Washington, the scene of her greatest glories and died in 1849.

James Monroe

—— five ——

James Monroe, the last of the elected Virginia presidents, was one of just two men whose popularity was so high that they were unopposed for reelection, the other being George Washington. In 1824, as his second term came to an end, the sixty-seven-year-old Monroe was tired after a lifetime of government service that began during the Revolutionary War. He briefly considered running for a third term, but knew that the two-term tradition was already well established.

As the end of his term approached, he began to look forward to it. He wrote to Jefferson, "I shall be heartily rejoiced when the term of my service expires, and I may return home in peace with my family, on whom, and especially on Mrs. Monroe, the burdens & cares of my long public service have borne too heavily."

When he turned the presidency over to John Quincy Adams on March 4, 1825, Monroe hoped to leave immediately for his estate, but his wife was ill, and he delayed leaving Washington for ten days. He remained at the White House.

His estate, Oak Hill, had been built during his presidency, a spacious mansion designed by Thomas Jefferson and surrounded by oak trees presented him by the states. The retirement he had longed for would not be the pleasant experience he had envisioned. From the start he was plagued by financial difficulties. From his service in the Revolutionary War through a series of government posts and finally to the presidency, his expenses were always greater than his salary, especially when he served as minister to France and Great Britain. Slowly, his once sizable fortune decreased. Several months before leaving the White House, he reviewed his financial records and found that not only were his resources nearly gone, he had sold several pieces of property to pay his creditors. He decided to ask the government for the money owed him and first wrote to Jefferson to gain support.

> In the settlement of the accounts of both my missions to Europe, that commencing in 1794 under Genl. Washington, and that of 1803 under you, I have thought that injustice was done me. . . . The period of my retirement approaching, I intend to invite the attention of Congress to both subjects. . . . It would be gratifying to me to be permitted by you to show to the Committee to whom the subject will probably be referred the first paragraph of your letter of the thirteenth of January, 1803, announcing to me my appointment. . . . The sole object . . . would be to show the haste with which I hurried from home; & from the country, leaving my private concerns in consequence unsettled.

To James Madison he also wrote asking for backing, stating that while he was serving in Europe, he was forced to sell 950 acres near Charlottesville, which might not have been necessary if he had been home.

His claims to Congress failed to bring action and just one month after leaving office Monroe was forced to sell 3,500 acres near Albemarle and 700 acres near Milton. Still, the parade of creditors would not end. In August, he wrote to a friend, "My land and slaves have all been sold in Albemarle, as has been the tract of 20,000 acres in Clay County, Ken., in satisfaction of debts contracted in the public service, and large balances are still due."

The creditors began to press. John Jacob Astor combined congratulations with a gentle press for repayment. "Permit me to congratulate you on your Honourable retirement. . . . Without wishing to cause you any Inconvenience (sic) on account of the loan which I so long since made to you I would be glad if you would put it in a train of sittlement (sic) if not the whole let it be a part with the interest Due."

His plight was desperate. He wrote to Jefferson that even if Congress were to pay the money he claimed, he could not pay all of his bills. Again he wrote Jefferson, "My debts abroad were great, and my plantations in Albemarle & here (Oak Hill) have added considerably to them every year, so that with accumulated loans and interest, compound added to simple, they have become immense."

Soon, Monroe learned that Jefferson, to whom he had complained about finances, was in even worse financial straits than he. Monroe joined in efforts to obtain money from the Virginia legislature for Jefferson. But his own concerns could not be forgotten for long. To Madison he wrote in 1828, "I have failed in the sale of my lands in this country, or any part thereof, and in consequence, being informed that there were several persons desirous of purchasing tho' not willing to give the price I asked, I have advertised both tracts for sale, to the highest bidder. . . ."

Still, Congress stalled on his request to be paid his just claims. Year after year, his request wound its way through committees, but in the end, the result was always the same, another delay. Finally, near desperation, he was ready to give up. In 1827 he wrote to a friend, "I shall never apply again to Congress, let my situation be what it may." Eventually, Congress did approve $30,000 which combined with his land sales satisfied all of his debts. But the money came as death approached, and could in no way repay the years of poverty Monroe had suffered. In 1831, he sold the estate he loved, Oak Hill. He had no land left, no place to call home.

In his retirement, he stayed away from politics, refusing to become involved in endorsing candidates or advising his successors. In 1826, there was a short-lived movement to draft him to serve as governor of Virginia once again. But he declined, citing his personal financial problems.

He did agree to serve with Madison as a member of a convention to rewrite the Virginia constitution. Monroe was elected president of the convention, but the delegates were unable to resolve the overwhelming differences between the Eastern and Western parts of the state, the slaveholding and the nonslaveholding areas.

On September 23, 1830, Mrs. Monroe died, and Monroe was overcome with grief. Her body remained in the house for several days as Monroe was unable to accept her death and delayed burying her.

With his wife gone, his assets nearly exhausted, Monroe decided to leave Virginia and move to New York City to live with his son-in-law and daughter in a modest house near the Bowery. He was a lonely man; neighborhood boys said hello to him each day as he walked to the docks but had no idea who he was. He lived quietly, breaking his silence only once, to appear at a New York rally to celebrate the dethronement of Charles X of France late in 1830.

His health became more of a problem, he apparently suffered from some type of tubercular condition. He wrote to his doctor, "I am free from pain, but my cough annoys me much, both day and night. . . ."

In an effort to raise money, he undertook two literary projects. The first was entitled, "A Biographical and Historical View of the Great Events to which Mr. Monroe was a Party and of which he was a Spectator in the Course of his Public Service." The second was entitled, "A Comparison of the American Republic with the Republics of Greece and Rome." He did some work on the first and nearly finished the second, which was published thirty-eight years later.

In the final years of his life, he was unable to see his old friends in Virginia. In what would be a farewell letter to Madison, he wrote, "It is very distressing to me to sell my property in Loudoun, for besides parting with all I have in the State, I indulged a hope, if I could retain it, that I might be able occasionally to visit it, and meet my friends, or many of them there." Monroe had given everything for his country, and in the end was left with nothing.

On July 4, 1831, Madison died. It was five years to the day since the death of Adams and Jefferson. He was seventy-three years old. There was a memorial service in New York attended by thousands of people. He was buried in the vault of his son-in-law's family, where he remained until his remains were moved to Richmond in 1858.

He left no estate.

John Quincy Adams

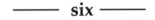

six

From the moment John Quincy Adams won the presidency, there were many who said he had stolen it, seized it from the rightful winner, Andrew Jackson. Jackson had won a plurality of both the popular and electoral vote, but with four candidates competing, could not muster the necessary majority. So, the election was decided by the House of Representatives, where Adams emerged the winner.

Just as his father worked under the shadow of George Washington, John Quincy Adams was doomed to serve under the shadow of the popular Jackson. After a single term, he was turned out by the voters. Of the first seven presidents, only two were rejected by the voters, John Adams, and his son, John Quincy Adams. John Quincy Adams had been unable to govern; both the Congress and the people realized that his election had been a fluke, and his chances for reelection nonexistent. Even Adams wrote before his defeat, "What retirement will be I cannot realize, but have formed no favorable anticipation. It cannot be worse than this perpetual motion and crazing cares. The weight grows heavier from day to day."

Following his crushing defeat by Jackson in 1828, Adams wrote, "The sun of my political career sets in the deepest gloom." As his term came to an end, he wrote, "Three days more, and I shall be restored to private life and left to an old age of retirement, though certainly not of repose. . . . I go into it with a combination of parties and public men against my character and reputation such as

I believe never before was exhibited against any man since the Union existed." His bitterness increased, directed at anyone he thought responsible for his loss. "No one knows, and few conceive the agony that I have suffered from the time that I was made by circumstances, and not by violation, a candidate for the presidency till I was dismissed from that station by the failure of my re-election. . . . It seemed as if I were deserted by all mankind. . . ."

Finally, in the depth of despair, he wrote in his diary, "I have no plausible motive for wishing to live, when everything that I foresee and believe of futurity makes death desireable."

After a lifetime of government service throughout the world, Adams had no true home and decided to remain in Washington. "It was my intention to bury myself in complete retirement as much as a nun taking the veil." His wife Louisa preferred not to see her husband's depression and told friends that he had never been happier. But his bitterness only increased as the days passed in his forced exile. He was shunned by official Washington and except for Secretary of State Martin Van Buren, no member of the Jackson Administration came to visit him and he said, "They hate the man they have wronged."

He tried his hand at writing fables, but was unhappy with the results. There were also increasing problems with his son, George, who was highly nervous and suffered from mental problems. He neglected the family's business forcing Adams to rebuke his son, "Time was when I took it for granted that your life was sober, regular and industrious, now I need weekly assurance." He suggested that George join a group dedicated to battling alcoholism, but did send his son $1,000 to pay anxious creditors.

George's mental condition grew worse; he became increasingly paranoid, imagining that people were breaking into his room, and he heard voices constantly. Finally, the demons in his head became too much. While traveling by steamship, he awoke during the night and began waking the other passengers, accusing them of conspiring against him. Then he disappeared. "In the wandering of his mind he had fallen overboard," Adams noted. He was overcome with grief such as "I never knew before."

As therapy, he began to write a book about political parties and took regular swims in the Potomac River, and he decided to return to the family home in Quincy, Massachusetts. There was nothing left for him in Washington.

He ignored politics, seldom looking at a newspaper. "Of public affairs I take no thought, I wish to dismiss them forever."

He had hoped for a quiet retirement, but his finances were precarious. Because of his investments, he had an income of $6,000 a year, but about one-third of that went to pay for his heavily mortgaged property. His income depended in large measure on the flour mills he owned. The mills depended on markets in Britain and France for success, but good harvests in those countries dried up the markets. He was forced to delay his return to Massachusetts in order to look after the mills. A quarter of a century earlier, John Quincy Adams had suggested to his father that he write an autobiography. Adams worked on the project sporadically but never got very far. John Quincy Adams decided that he would complete the project. But, like his father, John Quincy Adams was unable to complete the project.

Adams's son, Charles, thought his father was even more depressed in 1830 than he had been the year before. But by a twist of fate, it was the supporters of Jackson who brought Adams's spirits back. The Boston *Courier,* a Jacksonian newspaper, suggested that Adams be elected as a congressman. The *Courier* felt that such an election would eliminate Adams as a national force.

Most thought that Adams would reject the idea as beneath the dignity of a former president. But Adams did not see it that way. Despite opposition from his family, Adams saw the post not as a comedown, but as an honor. In the 1830 election, Adams easily won the election, capturing nearly three out of four votes. In his joy, he wrote, "My election as President of the United States was not half as gratifying to my inmost soul."

The new Congress would hold a brief organizing session in March, but Adams did not wait: he left almost immediately for Washington. One reason was that he was anxious to begin his new job, but he was also concerned about the financial state of his mills. They had lost $15,000 due to Adams's decision to speculate in flour. He thought a European crisis would push prices up, but when the crisis failed to materialize, Adams was struck with more flour than he could sell.

After a brief organizing session, the Congress did not meet again until December 5, 1831. Adams was named chairman of the committee on manufacture, although he had hoped to serve on the foreign affairs committee. Despite the disappointment, Adams loved his new duties, and his return to politics had once again fueled his ambition. In 1833, leaders of the anti-Masons urged Adams to run for governor. At first, he hesitated but then agreed to carry the party's banner. Adams hoped to win the nomination of the National Republican Party, but the party rejected Adams.

As the candidate of the anti-Masons, Adams refused to campaign and had distain for those who did. "This fashion of peddling for popularity by traveling round the country gathering crowds together, hawking for public dinners and sprouting empty speeches is growing into high fashion."

In the gubernatorial election, Adams finished second in the four candidate race. It was almost a replay of the 1828 presidential election. No candidate had a majority, so the race would be decided by the Massachusetts House of Representatives where the field would be narrowed to two candidates, then to the state senate where a winner would be chosen.

Adams had learned his lesson well; he had promised that unless he won a clear majority of the votes, he would not accept the office. Adams threw his support to the candidate of the National Republicans and returned to his seat in Congress.

His son, John, died, and again Adams was thrown into a period of despair, saying the loss had "almost broken his heart." He devoted more and more time to his work in Congress. It was so unusual for Adams to be away from his seat that the *National Intelligencer* reported an infrequent absence in 1836, caused by an abscess that swelled his leg, leaving him unable to move from his couch.

But generally his health was good. Each year he gained respect and power in the Congress, and, gradually, he found his issue. Slavery was already inflaming passions, although the Civil War was a quarter of a century away. Adams hated the institution but was reluctant to become involved in the growing debate. Slowly, almost hesitantly, he found himself emerging as one of the leaders of the antislavery movement, although he would never consider himself a true abolitionist.

His involvement began in a minor way. The House had a custom to allow representatives to present petitions from their constituents each Monday. Adams received a number of petitions protesting slavery, but Southern members forced through a gag rule preventing any petitions regarding the reduction or elimination of slavery from being presented.

To Adams, it was a deplorable situation. If a gag rule on slavery could be enforced, then it was possible that any subject could be put off limits. He decided that he would fight the gag rule, although it was often a lonely battle. Time after time, week after week, he rose to present petitions against slavery, and each time he was drowned out by protests from Southern congressmen and orders from the speaker to take his seat. He appealed for votes, and they went overwhelmingly against him. The abolitionists tried to recruit Adams to their cause, but he would not officially enlist, preferring to battle alone. He hated slavery, but knew that any sudden attempt to end it might also end the Union. When Congress adjourned at the end of 1837, Adams had achieved no victories, but had angered the Southerners.

His financial situation had grown worse, and although he was anxious to return to Quincy, he needed to raise money to pay a long list of creditors including his former valet who was owed $1,000.

The twenty-fifth Congress convened and with it came another tidal wave of antislavery petitions from Adams. Because of his role, he found himself deluged with petitions not only from his own district but from throughout the country. In one day, 31 petitions arrived in his office. On February 14, 1838, he set a record by presenting 350 petitions. Nearly half protested the gag rule, and nearly all of the rest opposed slavery. As always, Adams was not allowed to read the resolutions, but only to place them on a table where they languished.

He was getting nowhere, and in June he tried another tactic, beginning a series of speeches on slavery that lasted into July. In the end, he said, "I do believe slavery is a sin before the sight of God and that is the reason and the only insurmountable reason why we should not annex Texas to this Union."

The cause was slavery, but the immediate issue had become Texas and its admission to the Union as a slave state. Adams saw clearly that adding Texas to the Union would also add to the power of the slaveholding states and add vast new territory for slaveholders.

Although Adams deplored slavery, he had angered some abolitionists who wanted him to support the immediate end to slavery. In 1838, the abolitionists put up a candidate to oppose Adams. Their strategy was crafty; their candidate was a write in, whom they hoped would win because Adams's supporters, figuring he had no opposition on the ballot, would not vote. It nearly worked, Adams won by only a few hundred votes.

The new Congress convened, and, quickly, the gag rule was reimposed. Again, he presented his petitions without being allowed to read them, and again they were placed on a table and ignored.

On February 15, 1839, he offered three amendments to the Constitution to eventually outlaw slavery. They would eliminate hereditary slavery after 1842, eliminate all slavery after 1845, and prohibit the admission of any slave state except Florida. Like most of Adams's measures, this one went nowhere.

Congressmen were paid on a per diem basis, and because the first session of the twenty-fifth Congress met only briefly, Adams made very little money. He was forced to sell some of his Boston real estate to make ends meet.

In 1840, Martin Van Buren was defeated for reelection, and Adams observed the same phenomenon that had followed his defeat. The large crowds of admirers who had flocked to the White House to see Van Buren stopped coming after his defeat and turned their attention to the incoming president. "Nothing more uniformly exemplifies this propensity of human nature than the exit of a President of the United States."

It had been nearly 50 years since Adams had practiced law in Boston, but now, in the twilight of his life, he was called upon to return to the courtroom one final time. In an unusual case, a group of Blacks were found half starved on the ship *Amistad* off Long Island. They spoke little English, and it took officials a long time to piece together their story. The Blacks had been seized in Africa and transported to Havana on a Portuguese slave ship. It was a clear violation of Spanish law, which had eliminated the slave trade in its island possession. Using false papers, the slaves were being taken from Havana to another Cuban town when the slaves revolted, killing the captain and seizing the ship. For weeks, the ship sailed aimlessly along the Atlantic coast, finally coming to Long Island.

The Spanish claimed that the ship should be returned to its owners, and the slaves sent back to Havana. Van Buren was indifferent to the case and refused to help the Blacks. A committee was organized to help the slaves, who were being held in jail until their case was decided, and the committee members enlisted Adams to lead the fight.

A lower court ruled that the blacks should be turned over to the president and transported back to Africa. Van Buren did not like the decision and ordered it appealed; the higher court upheld it, and then Van Buren went to the Supreme Court. Adams agreed to serve as assistant counsel in arguments before the Supreme Court. He spoke to the court for nearly five hours on his first day, then came back for another four-hour speech. His voice was strong, and the court upheld the lower court rulings and went further, the slaves were to be set free. After years of fighting slavery, Adams had won his first victory.

When the new session of Congress opened in 1842, Adams was once again ready with his petitions, and Congress was once again ready to ignore them. But one of the petitions contained a timebomb for Adams. Forty-six citizens from Haverhill, Massachusetts, called for the Union to be dissolved and the submission of the petition brought angry cries to censure Adams. The censure resolution read in part, "the Hon. John Quincy Adams . . . in presenting for the consideration of the House of Representatives of the United States a petition praying the dissolution of the Union, has offered the deepest indignity to the House of which he is a member . . . and will, if this outrage be permitted to pass unrebuked and unpunished, have disgraced his country . . . for this insult . . . might well be held to merit expulsion from the national councils; and the House deem it an act of grace and mercy, when they only inflict upon him their severest censure. . . ."

For years, the Southerners had listened as Adams had rebuked them; now they had their chance for revenge. The case stirred the nation, and as the case was considered by the House, the galleries were packed. It looked as though the debate would last for weeks, as Adams and the Southerners traded charges on issues which dated back 25 years. Despite the fiery oratory from both sides, there were a number of attempts to reach a compromise. Finally, a Southerner moved to table the censure resolution and it passed by the narrow margin of 106 to 93. Not only had Adams escaped censure, but he had increased his national standing, especially among the abolitionists.

When the new Congress convened in 1843, Adams again introduced his resolution to allow the presentation of petitions regarding abolition. Again it failed, but this time the margin was just nine votes. Adams was getting closer. It encouraged him to become more outspoken. In a speech in Bangor, Maine, he said, "Are we not suffering our own hands to be manacled and our feet to be fettered with the chains of slavery?"

Again in 1844 Adams faced a strong opponent, so strong that he thought he would be defeated. Adams, however, won easily, capturing nearly 60 percent of the vote.

When the new Congress met in 1845, Adams again introduced his resolution against the gag rule. Again, as they had always done the Southerners moved to kill his resolution by tabling it. But this time, things were different. The motion to table failed; the Southerners had been defeated. Then Adams pushed his resolution, which passed by a wide margin. After eight years, Adams had won. "Blessed, forever, blessed be the name of God," Adams said.

He was reelected in 1846 by a margin of just 651 votes. He was seventy-nine years old and his health was becoming a greater concern. On November 20, shortly after the election, Adams went for a walk near his son's Boston home. Suddenly, Adams lost feeling in his legs and began to sink to the ground; a companion grabbed him and helped him back to his son's home. He had suffered a stroke affecting his speech and right side but slowly recovered, and in February returned to his home in Washington.

Back in Congress, Adams became one of the leaders of the movement fighting American participation in the Mexican War. He backed a resolution seeking to withdraw U.S. forces from Mexico and calling for negotiations with Mexico. Only three other representatives joined in supporting the resolution. Once again, Adams stood almost alone.

His opposition to the war continued, although for most of the nation, the war was popular and easily won. On January 21, 1848, Adams was in his seat as usual when a resolution was introduced to thank military officers for their service in the war. Adams shouted 'No' to the resolution; it was loud enough to be heard over the scores of yes votes.

Next, the House was asked to consider a resolution for the soldiers who had conquered Montezuma. Suddenly, Adams flushed, attempted to move his lips, but could not talk. He slumped over his desk, but a congressman sitting nearby caught Adams before he fell to the floor. He was carried on a sofa to the rotunda, then to the Speaker's chamber. Slowly, his mouth formed words, and he quietly said, "This is the last of the earth, I am content."

Adams remained in the Speaker's chamber until the twenty-third, never coming out of the coma. Then, he died.

Andrew Jackson

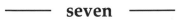

Andrew Jackson was old and tired when his second term came to an end in 1837. He was seventy years old and anxious to return to his Tennessee estate, the Hermitage. "The rest of my life is retirement and ease," he said. The trip home was a mixture of pleasure and pain. Along the route, crowds turned out to cheer Jackson, but he also saw growing economic troubles, caused by land speculation and an abundance of bank notes.

Jackson was one of those facing financial problems. He told a friend that he had returned home

> with barely ninety dollars in my pocket, bacon for my family and corn and oats for the stock to buy, and the new roof on my house just rebuilt leaking and to be repaired. I carried $5,000 when I went to Washington; it took my cotton crop, $2,250, with my salary, to bring me home. The burning of my house and furniture has left me poor.

The failing economy had been particularly hard on Tennessee; some state banks failed while others united in an effort to survive. As the financial panic grew, so did the criticism of Jackson's financial policies and those of his hand picked successor, Martin Van Buren.

Despite the criticism, Jackson urged Van Buren to stand firm against the speculators and overextended bankers who wanted the government to provide relief in the form of cheap money. He wrote to Van Buren saying, "The eyes of the people are fast opening," and telling him to fight on. "Be ye therefore steady, firm and un-wavering in your course and all is safe."

Jackson's financial problems came not only from the Panic of 1837, but from his son, Andrew Jackson, Jr. Young Jackson went from one financial disaster to another. Like other land owners, Jackson adhered to the custom of paying off all bills on each January first. At the beginning of 1838, Jackson was able to pay his bills only by selling some of his land in West Tennessee. "I have no opinion of holding property when I need the money, and I will not borrow. . . . Since last spring we have paid upwards of seven thousand dollars."

Most of the $7,000 went to pay off debts for young Jackson. He had endorsed notes for others, and when they were unable to pay, the creditors turned to young Jackson who turned to his father. Each time, Jackson urged his son to avoid financial prob-lems, and each time, Jackson junior promised him that he would never again get in over his head. Jackson never lost faith in his son, refusing to believe that it was his son's fault. "Andrew was inex-perienced, and he happened to fall into the hands of men who pre-tended to be his friends." To pay his bills, he pressed those who owed him money and threatened to turn the collection over to an attorney.

One by one, his friends died, and Jackson's health was not good. His eyesight was failing, and his memory was fading. He wrote, "Had I a wish to travel I have now no one to go with me." He had hoped that 1838 would bring the return to good economic times. Jackson was able to keep the Hermitage profitable, but he continued to supply his son with a never-ending supply of money. He paid over $5,000 for a downpayment for a plantation for young Jackson, but young Jackson's management abilities were poor.

When Van Buren invited Jackson to attend ceremonies mark-ing the twenty-fifth anniversary of the Battle of New Orleans, Jackson replied, "Again I am out of funds, and I cannot bear to bor-row or travel as a pauper."

He received yet another bill from one of his son's creditors, this one seeking $550 for a carriage young Jackson had purchased. Almost at the end of his wits, Jackson wrote the creditor, "I have exerted all my means to clear . . . (Andrew) from his foolish as well as useless debts. . . . They are all exhausted, I can do no more."

Despite his words, Jackson would continue to bail his son out of trouble. Finally, he was forced to borrow $3,000 to meet his son's bills. In 1840, Jackson sold 3 lots in Florence, Alabama to raise $240 to pay more of young Jackson's bills. The money came just in time to prevent the sheriff from arresting the young man for nonpayment of debts. Finally, in desperation, Jackson asked his son for a complete list of all of his debts. Andrew figured that he owed nearly $6,000. Jackson went to New Orleans to secure a line of credit to pay the youth's bills. He thought he would bring an end to Andrew's problems forever. He was wrong, soon learning that his son's bills totaled not $6,000, but $12,000. He paid $11,000 worth and promised the creditors the rest would be paid within a short time. Again, it turned out that not all of Andrew's bill had been paid. Jackson wrote to his son, "Sell all (the beef) you can spare. . . . Sell the fillies if you can get five hundred dollars for the two in cash. If you can get as much for my riding mare as two hundred dollars let her go and pay . . . what you owe."

As the 1840 election approached, it was clear Van Buren was in trouble. His support of Jackson's policies, coupled with the national recession had severely damaged his popularity. The Whigs put forward William Henry Harrison, who, they hoped, would remind the voters of Jackson. Jackson had pushed Van Buren for the presidency in 1836, and now wanted to see him reelected. He campaigned for Van Buren, but it was a lost cause.

When New Year's Day came in 1841, Jackson could not pay his bills, as he had done every year of his adult life. In fact, he was unable to figure out how much he owed. The original $6,000 debt of young Jackson turned into $15,000, and still Jackson was not sure there would be no more. As usual, Jackson blamed his son's problems on others. He said the debts were the result of a swindle perpetrated on young Andrew.

Jackson had given so much for his son, that the Hermitage began to look neglected, in need of paint and repair. Gradually, word of Jackson's financial problems became public. His 1841 cotton crop failed and his seven prize horses died. Friends floated a series of plans to give Jackson money, but he was too proud to accept gifts, but he would accept loans. Francis Blair, one of Jackson's advisors, wrote offering a loan of $25,000, which Jackson quickly accepted. But he insisted on giving Blair a mortgage on his son's plantation and included a codicil in his will that Blair would be repaid before any bequests were made.

Once again, Jackson believed he had finally solved his financial problems, but as 1842 began, he found himself in the same situation as in 1841. He had shipped his cotton to England, hoping to realize a larger profit that he could in New Orleans but the scheme backfired. The cotton brought no more than he could have obtained in New Orleans, and the shipping charges consumed most of the money he did receive. He was forced to ask Blair to delay the first payment on his loan. The next two years began the same way; Jackson could not pay his debts.

Eighteen forty-four also brought another presidential election and Jackson's protégé hoped to return to the White House. Jackson was determined to see a Democrat elected. The election of William Henry Harrison in 1840 had upset him, and when Harrison died shortly after taking office, Jackson was overjoyed. "A kind and overruling providence, has interfered to prolong our glorious union and happy republican system which Gen. Harrison and his cabinet were preparing to destroy . . . let the people rejoice." Van Buren's decision to oppose the annexation of Texas cost him Jackson's support and gave the nomination to James K. Polk, a fellow Tennessean and close friend. He was so close to Jackson that his nickname became "Young Hickory."

Polk's victory meant that Jackson had been able to put two of his protégés in the White House. Polk's election brought out the job seekers, many of whom turned to Jackson. "I am dying as fast as I can, and they know it, but they will keep swarming upon me in clouds, seeking office, intriguing for office." When Polk rejected some of Jackson's recommendations, Jackson became angry and wrote him on the subject of ingratitude.

Jackson could influence the nation, but he could not pay his bills. His health became more fragile and he became despondent. To one friend he wrote, "I await with resignation the call of my God," and to another he said, "Poverty stares us in the face."

He had to ask his creditors to delay his payments, and, once again, Blair came to the rescue, telling Jackson he was authorized to borrow as much as $100,000 from his firm. The letter brought tears to the old man's eyes. When Jackson went over his son's accounts again and found the boy owed another $8,000, he borrowed that amount, thinking he had finally solved young Andrew's problems.

His health continued to decline and he wrote to Polk, "My lamp is nearly burned out, and the last glimmer has come." He was blind in one eye and could no longer lie down, sitting up in bed propped up with pillows. Death was near, but once again Jackson had to face a new debt for young Andrew who had overdrawn his account. Jackson wrote to the creditor, "You may rest assured that A. Jackson Jnr will never again draw unless covered by assets. . . ."

On Thursday, June 5, 1845, Jackson's daughter, Sarah, sat beside his bed and asked him how he felt. "Pretty comfortable, but I cannot be long with you all. I wish to be buried without display or pomp, or any superfluous expense."

The next morning he said he wanted to write a letter to Polk. His son suggested that he wait until the next day, but Jackson said, "Tomorrow, I may not be here."

On Sunday, June 8, Jackson said farewell to his family and servants. "My dear children, and friends, and servants, I hope and trust to meet you all in Heaven, both white and black, both white and black." At six o'clock he died at the age of seventy-eight.

Martin Van Buren

—— eight ——

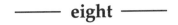

The rise of Martin Van Buren was dramatic: U.S. senator, governor of New York, secretary of state, U.S. minister to England, vice-president and finally president, all within 16 years. He had chosen his political friends well, and when he aligned himself with Andrew Johnson, his future was assured. Johnson made Van Buren vice-president and in 1837 delivered the Democratic nomination to his protégé.

But Van Buren lacked the popular appeal of a Jackson, and when the Panic of 1837 began, his popularity faded. He had enough strength to regain the nomination in 1840, but he was no march for the aging war hero, William Henry Harrison. The popular vote was reasonably close (Harrison received 53 percent) but Van Buren trailed badly in the electoral vote.

Van Buren took his defeat well, perhaps because at the age of fifty-eight he believed he would be able to make a comeback. He returned to his home in upstate New York and along the way received warm welcomes. In New York City, 8,000 people turned out to cheer him.

His wealth made it possible for him to live the life of a country gentleman. Almost from the day he returned home he began writing a steady stream of letters to politicians around the country. He did not want to be forgotten, even though he told his neighbors, "I come to take up my final residence with you." He had purchased the Peter Van Ness estate with its 200 acre farm and 30-room mansion. Within a month, events began to turn Van Buren's way. Harrison died and later in the year, the Democrats regained control of the New York legislature with Van Buren's supporters making the greatest gains. He was well positioned for another try for the presidential nomination. He had thought that politicians would come to his estate seeking his advice, but no one came, and he soon realized that he would have to go looking for support. He made a trip to Tennessee to visit his mentor, Andrew Jackson. But the trip had another purpose: Van Buren was going to visit Henry Clay in Kentucky. If Van Buren had the edge for the Democratic nomination in 1844, Clay had all but a lock on the Whig nomination. Their two-day meeting would end forever the chance that either would ever become president.

The dominant issue in the 1844 campaign would be the annexation of the Republic of Texas into the United States. It was a volatile issue, opposed by many in the North who saw it as a device to bring another slave state into the Union, while others feared it would lead to a war with Mexico.

No matter which side a candidate chose, he was certain to lose some support. In one of the most unusual political deals ever made, Clay and Van Buren agreed to ignore the issue. They believed that they could somehow keep the issue from dominating the campaign simply by not talking about it. As the 1844 Democratic convention approached, a Richmond newspaper published a letter from Jackson stating that he supported annexation of Texas. Van Buren had a choice: follow the lead of the man who had made him president or stick to his agreement with Clay. In a fatal mistake, he and Clay both published letters opposing annexation of Texas. Immediately, Jackson fell away and informed his backers that he favored the nomination of an proannexation candidate.

Van Buren still had the support of more than half the delegates, but could not gain the two-thirds majority needed to win the nomination. Van Buren's support began to fade and on the second day, the convention nominated James K. Polk, a man with unimpressive political credentials, but a man who had the backing of Jackson.

Van Buren masked his disappointment and campaigned for Polk. He hoped to gain influence with the new administration but again was disappointed. He wanted Polk to give his supporters key government posts, but came away empty handed. Polk did offer Van Buren's followers some minor roles, but an angry Van Buren told them not to accept.

For every former president, there is a point when he realizes that power has clearly passed. For most, it is the day after the election; others sense it on the day their successor is inaugurated. For Van Buren, the realization came when he instructed his supporters not to accept the positions in the Polk administration. They knew that Van Buren's days as a power in the Democratic Party were over, and they rushed to accept the Polk offer.

What Polk wanted most was to get Van Buren out of the way. He devised a plan to offer the former president his old post as minister to Great Britain. But Van Buren saw the offer for what it was; in fact, Van Buren had tried the same trick, offering the same post to DeWitt Clinton to remove him as a political force. Just as Clinton had done, Van Buren declined the offer, still hoping that some day he would be able to reclaim the White House.

Van Buren had fallen prey to a political phenomenon that would stretch from Jackson's administration to the election of Abraham Lincoln. Men like Clay, John Calhoun, and Daniel Webster were men with well-known political convictions, and although they were qualified to be president, their convictions would hamper them. To take a strong stand risked the loss of support from either North or South, so the political parties turned to men whose views were largely unknown. Van Buren fit that description until he took sides on the annexation issue.

Denied a national forum, Van Buren returned to the surroundings that launched his early career, New York politics. Once he had spoken out against annexation of Texas, the die was cast, and he had nothing to lose by coming out strongly against the expansion of slavery. His enemies and those who supported the expansion of slavery said he was like the farmer who burned down his barn to eliminate the rats. He and his followers were nicknamed Barnburners, and the name implied that they would be willing to see the Union go up in flames over the slavery issue. Van Buren told friends, "The end of slavery will come amid terrible convulsions, I fear, but it will come."

Polk saw the Van Buren movement as a threat to the future of the Democratic party and moved to undercut the Barnburners. He began offering government jobs to Van Buren's supporters, taking away some of his key backing. But Van Buren retained enough strength to field a delegation to the 1848 Democratic National Convention in Baltimore. The regular Democrats also sent a delegation, and the party, seeking to avoid disunity, decided to seat both delegations. But the Barnburners were unwilling to join with the regular slate and walked out of the convention.

Van Buren's supporters formed the Free Soil Party and nominated the former president as its candidate. The Democrats nominated Lewis Cass of Michigan and the Whigs selected Zachary Taylor, a former military leader.

Van Buren's new party, dedicated to the elimination of slavery, had no chance of winning the election, but he could extract a measure of revenge on the party which had turned against him. He won just 10 percent of the vote, but it came from the states the Democrats had counted on for victory. Van Buren's fledgling party had placed the Whigs back in the White House. He was the first of three former presidents who attempted to recapture the White House through a third party. (The other two were Millard Fillmore in 1856 and Theodore Roosevelt in 1912.) Van Buren polled the smallest percentage of the three, but along with Roosevelt had the greatest impact.

Even Van Buren now knew that his political career was over. He played no role in the election of 1852 and left for Europe. He was the first former president to travel abroad visiting England, France, Switzerland, Belgium, Holland, and finally settling in the Italian city of Sorrento where he started to write his memoirs. His memoirs began, "At the age of seventy-one, and in a foreign land, I commence a sketch of the principal events of my life." He told a friend he was writing the book "to vindicate my administration."

He also started writing a history of the nation's political parties. In 1856, his son, Martin, died, and Van Buren returned to the United States, bringing an end to his literary projects.

He returned to the Democratic party in 1856 to support James Buchanan, but his endorsement was not a factor in the election. He had become a forgotten man, his administration dismissed as overly political and blundering. In 1862, Van Buren was seventy-nine years old, a feeble figure who spent his time in his house, unable to do more than sit in a chair. On July 24, Van Buren died, alone.

John Tyler

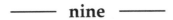

—— **nine** ——

William Henry Harrison served as president for just one month and when the aging general died, John Tyler of Virginia became the first vice-president to succeed to the presidency. It was an awkward time for the nation; there was some confusion as to just what Tyler's job would be. Many saw him only as an "acting president," and were unsure what powers he had inherited. It did not bother Tyler who assumed all responsibilities of the presidency.

His major problem, however, was that he was a man without a political party. Tyler, a Democrat, had been elected on the Whig ticket as a device to gather Southern votes; the Whigs considered him a Democrat, and the Democrats thought him to be a Whig. Tyler realized that neither party would give him the presidential nomination in 1844, despite his desire to serve a full term. He believed that Martin Van Buren and Henry Clay would win their parties' nominations and he thought both men were weak on his favorite issue, state's rights.

Tyler hit upon a scheme to form a third-party movement, even though he knew he could not win. His idea was to use his candidacy as a device to get one of the major parties to nominate a candidate more to his liking. Van Buren was denied the nomination, although Tyler played no part in the process. But Tyler thought he had more power than he actually did, and agreed to drop out of the race, thinking he and Polk had agreed to give Tyler a role in the new administration. Two days before Polk's inauguration, Tyler and his wife Julia moved out of the White House and into a hotel.

Tyler's first wife had died, and he had married Julia eight months earlier. The morning after the inauguration, they went to the docks to take a boat down the Potomac River heading toward their Virginia plantation. When they arrived the boat had already left and they had to return to their hotel, an embarrassing moment after the emotional sendoff they had received. Tyler was learning the first lesson for former presidents; the boat waits for presidents, but not for expresidents.

Tyler returned to his 1,150 acre estate on the James River near Richmond. It was called The Grove, but Tyler renamed it Sherwood Forest, seeing himself as Robin Hood mistreated by his political opponents who were the Sheriff of Nottingham. His neighbors, mostly Whigs, gave him a chilly reception and in an effort to humiliate him, elected him as overseer of roads for the county, a job just one step above dog catcher. They meant it as a joke, but it was Tyler who had the laugh. The overseer was a plantation owner who decided which roads were to be repaired and when. Usually, the work was done during the off season by slaves, although the overseer of roads had the right to call the slaves together at any time. Tyler called the slaves out at the height of the harvest season, making it hard for the owners to get their crops in. Finally, the plantation owners came to Tyler and asked him to resign from his office. He replied, "Offices are hard to obtain in these times, and having no assurance that I will ever get another, I could not think under the circumstances of resigning."

It was one of the few humorous moments Tyler was to have. Once James Polk was safely in the White House, he quickly forgot any promises he might have made to Tyler. The former president could not even secure a diplomatic appointment for his son, Robert. His family still nurtured hopes that Tyler would one day return to the White House, although nearly everyone else had written him off.

In 1848, Tyler, at the urging of his politically minded if inept son, Alexander, went to New York, hoping to stir up some support for a possible presidential bid. Unfortunately for Tyler, his political stock had fallen so low that the newspapers reported that he was in New York to line up support for Zachary Taylor. The New York *Herald* added another insult, "That once distinguished man, whom the steamboat left on the wharf . . . has long since ceased to possess any influence for either good or evil."

Tyler's dislike of Polk increased, and the election of Taylor pleased Tyler, even though he had voted for the Democratic candidate, Lewis Cass. Taylor, like Tyler, was a slaveholder and would not tamper with the institution Tyler respected above all others. In Taylor, Tyler saw yet another chance to line up at the patronage trough to secure jobs for his relatives. He pushed forward his son, John, his brother-in-law, his wife's cousin, and others. But Tyler had no better luck with Taylor than Polk; his relatives remained on the outside.

Tyler passed his time as a gentleman farmer, presiding over his estate and its 60 slaves. His wife, Julia, 30 years younger than her husband, came from a wealthy family and brought enough money to the marriage to insure that Tyler was financially secure. His family occupied a great deal of his time: he had seven children by his first marriage and seven by his second.

There were only a handful of visits from political leaders seeking his advice, even though Tyler and his wife still hoped that his political career might not be over. In 1852, his wife wrote that friends were ready to put Tyler's name into nomination if the Democratic convention became deadlocked. Again, in 1856, Tyler hoped that the nation might turn to him, even though there was no evidence he had any support outside his family.

As the 1860 political season approached, Tyler came up with two schemes. First, he envisioned a Democratic ticket with his old friend, Virginia governor, Henry Wise, for president and Tyler's son, Robert, for vice-president. It was pure folly; Wise was so radical in his views on slavery that he was even rejected by the voters of Virginia when he sought reelection in 1859. Robert Tyler, like his brother, Alexander, and their father, spent his life chasing one political dream after another with little success. He had become chairman of the Pennsylvania Democratic party, but had never run for elective office.

Tyler's second scheme was that somehow he might win the Democratic nomination. Robert, meanwhile, was pushing his father for the nomination and Tyler claimed that he had, "daily assurances from plain men of an anxious desire on their part to restore me to the presidency." It was clear that the Democrats would be badly divided and he thought he might somehow be able to pick up the pieces. On the evening of the convention, Tyler said, "I verily believe that I should at this day meet with more enthusiasm from the rank and file than has occurred since Jackson's time."

There was nothing behind the Tyler effort, and Tyler, finally realizing how ridiculous his situation was, withdrew from the race. Abraham Lincoln won the election, and events began to move quickly, state after state leaving the Union. Tyler, the eternal optimist, decided to step into the crisis.

Tyler proposed to call the 12 border states together to try to find a compromise. He reasoned that without the support of these states, neither North nor South would be able to obtain the upper hand. But even in making the proposal, Tyler was careful to lay the groundwork for secession. He said that if the conference failed, the Southern states should be free to go their own way. After that, his plan became so twisted, that few could even figure it out. He suggested that the secessionist states should adopt a constitution identical to the U.S. Constitution, except for some provisions protecting slavery. The secessionist states would then invite the remaining members of the Union to join them in forming a new union.

Tyler's plan was so confusing that it became impossible to tell who was succeeding. His peace convention idea grew to include all states, and he was selected as one of Virginia's delegates to the conference. For Tyler and his wife, it would be their first trip to Washington since they left 15 years before. Julia, the society lover, looked upon the trip as an opportunity to once again be at the center of the exciting parties after years of isolation at Sherwood Forest.

The peace conference opened in February, but it was already too late to reverse the Southern position. Tyler, nearly seventy-one, was elected president of the conference, but it turned into a tragic circus. Tyler, in poor health, was in over his head and his wife Julia saw the entire conference as an opportunity to attend parties and once again climb the social ladder. From the beginning, the conference was doomed, the debate was disorderly, and Tyler could not control the delegates.

Tyler began to despair that any compromise could be reached. He thought that one or two Northern states would join with the Southern states to form a new nation, making it impossible for the North to mount a serious war effort. The conference began to fall apart, and Tyler did nothing to bring it together. His main goals were preserving slavery and protecting Virginia from war.

The conference came up with a hodgepodge of recommendations aimed at preserving slavery through changes in the Constitu-

tion. Tyler told the conference he would submit the recommendations, but he was in too much of a hurry to return to Richmond for
the secession debates. He merely forwarded the recommendations
to Congress where they died. Tyler, the father of the peace conference and its president, returned to Richmond to deliver a fiery
speech denouncing the work of the conference. He called for Virginia to secede and then took his seat as a representative to the secession debates.

In the debates, he spoke for hours, a combination of fire-
breathing oratory and dreams. He said that if Virginia left the
Union, it would influence Northern states to follow. He said that
New Jersey, Pennsylvania, and even New York City would join the
Confederacy.

Virginia left the Union and Tyler was offered a seat in the provisional congress of the Confederate States of America. But his
health was too fragile to permit a trip to the session in Montgomery, Alabama. The Confederate government moved to Richmond,
and Tyler was given another chance to serve, winning a seat in the
Confederate Congress by an overwhelming margin. Tyler was
back in politics with a new nation.

The reality of the Civil War came quickly for the Tylers; his
property at Old Pont Comfort was seized in the early days of the
war when the Union troops reinforced Fort Monroe. Just two
months after the start of the war, Tyler began to talk of evacuating
his family to the Western area of the state.

During the first week of 1862, Tyler left Sherwood Forest for
Richmond to take his seat in the new Confederate Congress. His
wife remained behind, planning to join him later. When she arrived in Richmond several days later, she found her husband com-
plaining that he did not feel well. On the morning of January 17,
Tyler began vomiting, but later said he was feeling better. When he
stood up, he collapsed, but his primary concern was not his health,
but his absence from the first session of the new congress. But he
decided to return home to rest at Sherwood Forest. Hours before
he was to leave, his wife was awakened by the sound of her husband gasping for air. A doctor was summoned and Tyler told him,
"Doctor, I am going."

The doctor said, "I hope not Sir."

"Perhaps it is best," Tyler said. He looked at his wife, smiled,
then died.

His wife lived until 1889. There was a great deal of animosity between the children of his first and second marriages, and the eldest children never did meet the youngest. His first child was born in 1816, and his youngest child did not die until 1935.

James K. Polk

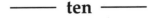

When James K. Polk became president in 1845, he was just forty-nine years old. The Democrats nominated Polk as a compromise candidate when the convention became deadlocked, and he dedicated his entire administration to a single theme, expansion. He pushed plans to acquire New Mexico and California from Mexico, and when Mexico rejected his plans, he declared war. At the same time, he negotiated with Britain to purchase the Oregon Territory and made an attempt to buy Cuba from Spain.

The war with Mexico and the increasingly bitter arguments between North and South combined to age him dramatically. James Buchanan said, "He was the most laborious man I have ever known; and in a brief period of four years had assumed the appearance of an old man."

From the beginning of his term, Polk made it clear that he would not be a candidate for a second term. There were some pressures from within his own party for Polk to run again, but he rejected them. The election of Zachary Taylor, the Whig nominee, disappointed Polk, who saw it as a rejection of his policies. Nevertheless, on the day Taylor was inaugurated, Polk wrote in his diary, "I feel exceedingly relieved that I am now free from all public cares. I am sure I shall be a happier man in my retirement than I have been during the four years I have filled the highest office in the gift of my countrymen."

Polk planned to spend his retirement in Tennessee where he had purchased a mansion in Nashville after selling his small family home in Columbia. At the age of fifty-three, he estimated that he would live another quarter of a century, but Polk's life could now be measured in weeks.

On Tuesday, March 6, 1849, Polk left Washington by steamboat, beginning the ordeal that would contribute to his death. He switched to a train and at Fredericksburg, Virginia, was met by his first welcoming party. He greeted the crowd and the train traveled another 30 miles where another group welcomed him and asked that he appear before a special session of the legislature in Richmond. He agreed, although he was becoming increasingly tired and coming down with a cold. In Petersburg, another group welcomed him and again he made a speech and had dinner.

Even in the small community of Weldon, North Carolina, he found a large group and wrote in his diary that "The principal hotel and other buildings of the place [were] brilliantly illuminated. This is a region of tar and turpentine, and bonfires were blazing in the streets."

The next day there was another reception, this one in Wilmington, and two days later another in Charleston, South Carolina. The reception ran late and Polk wrote in his diary, "I had left snow and ice at Washington not four days ago, and now I found myself in the midst of summer heat. This sudden transition from cold to heat, and the great fatigue I had endured during the day made the rest of the night very acceptable to me."

There was a reception in Savannah, Georgia, and another in Macon, and at every town in between, citizens came to the train station to see the former president. By the time Polk arrived in Montgomery, he was suffering from a violent cold. In Mobile, he cut short his reception at a theater, leaving after just 30 minutes to return to his hotel to rest.

In New Orleans another welcome added to the strain on Polk. In his diary he wrote that the welcoming party took him on a long procession. "I did not note the precise time but should guess it was between three and four hours from the time the procession moved from the railroad depot until I was taken to the quarters provided for me at the St. Louis Hotel. I was covered with dust and perspiration. I retired to my room for an hour and changed my dress. I feared the effects of the exposure to the sun and the excessive fatigue I had endured."

From New Orleans, Polk moved up the Mississippi River, but his condition was growing steadily worse, and he began to decline invitations from cities along the river to be a guest. On March 27, Polk arrived in Memphis, the first time he had been in his home state in more than four years. He could not refuse the welcoming committee from his home state, but came to regret it later. "I very soon felt the ill effects of the exertion through which I had imprudently gone. I found that the indisposition which had afflicted me for several days was increased."

Polk arrived at his new home in Nashville on April 2, his health nearly ruined by the long journey home, and now he was too weak to fight back. On June 15, just 15 weeks after leaving the White House, Polk died.

His wife, Sally, survived for nearly three decades. In 1876, Congress granted her a pension of $1,500 a year and raised it to $5,000 six years later.

Millard Fillmore

—— eleven ——

Millard Fillmore was yet another in the line of undistinguished presidents that stretched to the election of Abraham Lincoln. In 1848, the Whigs nominated Fillmore as their vice-presidential candidate to run with General Zachary Taylor. The Whigs needed Fillmore to help them carry New York, even though there was little to qualify him for the post.

Two years later, Fillmore became president when Taylor died. Two months after becoming president, Fillmore signed into law the Compromise of 1850, which was designed to preserve the Union through a series of compromises over slavery. The compromise only served to inflame the abolitionists who set up the underground railway to aid runaway slaves.

The compromise ruined both Fillmore and his party; the Whigs would never again win the presidency. But Fillmore could not see that he and his party were doomed. The strong antislavery element of the Whig party opposed the compromise including its hated fugitive slave provisions.

Throughout his career, Fillmore had been indecisive at crucial times, and, as the 1852 Whig convention approached, he could not decide whether to make a push for the nomination. This, coupled with reluctance on the part of many Whigs to give Fillmore the nomination, critically weakened his candidacy. Finally, Fillmore agreed to run "with sincere reluctance to their entreaties to suffer my name to remain before the public as a possible candidate." He believed that his control of the political patronage would be enough to ensure his nomination.

On the first ballot, Fillmore led with 133 votes, but General Winfield Scott was close behind with 131 votes, and Webster had 29. The Webster vote was particularly galling to Fillmore. Webster was his secretary of state but had broken with Fillmore for one last try for the presidency.

Fillmore's strength came from the South, which had gained the most from the Compromise of 1850. The balloting continued, but no candidate was able to gain a majority. Fillmore had given his convention manager a letter of withdrawal to be read if it appeared his candidacy was lost. Fillmore's friends worked to get Webster to drop out in favor of Fillmore. Finally, Webster agreed to withdraw and sent a note to Fillmore. "I have sent a communication to Baltimore this morning to have an end put to the pending controversy. I think it most probable you will be nominated before 1 o'clock. . . ."

But Fillmore replied that he had asked also that his name be withdrawn. "Your communication . . . I apprehend . . . may be too late to effect anything," he wrote Webster.

Webster's convention managers either did not receive his message or ignored it. When Webster supporters began to desert, they went not to Fillmore but to Scott. On the fifty-third ballot, Scott was nominated. The Whigs had returned to form. They had won the White House twice with military heroes, and they thought it might work a third time. It did not. Scott was humiliated in the election, carrying just four states.

With the election over, and his term coming to an end, Fillmore began planning his return to Buffalo, writing to a friend to "look around Buffalo for a suitable house for me." His home in Buffalo had been a modest frame house, and he did not want to return there. Other men who held the presidency had family wealth to fall back on, but Fillmore had always depended upon his salary. He was worth nearly $75,000, a large sum in 1852 but not enough to support himself in the style befitting a former president. He needed a job, but would not accept a position he thought beneath his dignity. He briefly considered accepting a job as a bank president but finally decided to return to practicing law.

Inauguration Day came, and after Franklin Pierce took the oath of office, Fillmore returned to the White House and then left for the Willard Hotel one block away. He was anxious to leave Washington, but the next morning, his wife came down with a severe cold, and his departure was delayed. Slowly, her life slipped away, and three weeks later she died.

He returned to Buffalo, but changed the plans he had made. With this wife gone, there would be no need for a greater income, and he dropped plans to resume his law practice. "My colleagues at the bar would say, and quite naturally, 'Here you have been to the pinnacle and ought to be content.'"

He purchased the Hollister House, a spacious home in downtown Buffalo. His return to Buffalo came as a new political movement began to grow. It started as a secret organization opposed to Catholics and immigrants and dedicated to seeing that all political offices were occupied by native-born Americans. The movement had its own passwords, secret handshakes, and system of rank. By 1854, it had become a political party and began fielding candidates. It was named the "American Party" but generally called the "Know-Nothing Party" because of the secret nature of its members.

Without any work to occupy his time, Fillmore became increasingly bored, and he was concerned about the growing threat of disunity. He also complained about the treatment accorded former presidents, writing that it was unfortunate they should "be cast adrift," when their terms ended.

In March 1854, he decided to tour the country, visiting prominent Whigs and seeking to learn if he had any support for another presidential bid. The trip was a success. In Ohio large crowds greeted him and there were receptions in Columbus and Cincinnati. The tour went through the South and he returned to Buffalo with the feeling that his political career might not be over.

If Fillmore found that his own standing remained high with many people, he must have also sensed that his party, the Whigs, were all but finished as a national power. He needed a party, and the Know-Nothings needed a leader with national stature. But the Know-Nothings had never been tested in an election, and before Fillmore would commit himself, he wanted to make sure that they could deliver votes. In 1854, the Know-Nothing movement grew rapidly, and in the fall elections scored impressive victories. They elected 17 congressmen, showing strength in the North and South. Fillmore became convinced he could use the Know-Nothings to establish a national party for his own return to power.

In July 1854, his twenty-two-year-old daughter died suddenly and Fillmore was overcome with grief. Since the death of his wife two years earlier, Mary Abigail Fillmore had responsibility for running her father's house. Fillmore, perhaps to forget his grief, devoted himself even more to politics.

On the first day of 1855, he told his friends that he was ready to run for president on the Know-Nothing ticket. "I have for a long time looked with dread and apprehension at the corrupting influence which the contest of the foreign vote is exciting upon our election." He decried the shame of filling political positions "by men of foreign birth to the exclusion of the native-born." He called for limiting the right to hold office to those "reared in a free country."

With his decisions made, Fillmore left for a 12-month tour of Europe, stopping in England, Ireland, France, Italy, Prussia, Turkey, and Egypt. He left behind his new political party to organize his campaign. In England, he turned down an honorary doctorate at Oxford, explaining that, "In my judgment, no man should accept a degree that he cannot read."

After a year, he returned to the United States and found the Know-Nothings in the midst of a crisis. A political party can be built on a single issue, as the Know-Nothings did on immigration, but once it tries to become a national force it must take positions on a wide range of issues and risk losing supporters. The issue for the Know-Nothings was slavery. Opponents of the Know-Nothings, seeking support for their new Republican Party, infiltrated the Know-Nothings and demanded that the party take a stand on the slavery issue.

The Republicans hoped that the issue would destroy the party and deliver its supporters into their party. The Republicans wanted the party to adopt a platform supporting the right of Congress to limit slavery. When the Know-Nothings refused, the infiltrators walked out, branding the party a pawn for the supporters of slavery. Fillmore was not entirely comfortable with his new party, and the signs of strain began to show. He was not anti-Catholic and had never had much of a taste for the crusade against the foreign-born. The result was a mellowing of the party, which cost it support during the summer of 1856. Against the fevered pitch of the Republicans and Democrats, the Fillmore effort was staid. Despite the strong showing in 1854, the Know-Nothings lacked the professional political managers to give the Fillmore campaign the organization it desperately needed.

With every third party effort, the favorable signs of spring gave way to the realities of fall. As election day approached, both

Republican and Democratic backers called on the Fillmore supporters to desert the Know-Nothings, rather than waste their votes.
The Democrats charged that a vote for Fillmore would aid the Republicans. The ploy worked especially well in the South.

On Election Day, Fillmore came in third behind the Democrat,
James Buchanan, and the Republican, John Fremont. He received
28 percent of the vote, primarily because of his appeal to the slaveholding states, which gave him more than half of his votes.

The size of the defeat surprised Fillmore, although he knew he
would lose. "Personally, I have nothing to regret in the results. . . . I
envy my successful rival; but sincerely hope that . . . [he] may so
discharge the . . . duties of his exalted station as to restore peace
and harmony."

He along with everyone else realized his position. "I consider
my political career at an end and have nothing further to ask," he
told a friend. "I profess to belong to no party but my country, and
am taking no part in politics . . . ." Fillmore had carried only Mary-
land and the election marked the beginning of the end for the
Know-Nothings. Fillmore had the distinction of being the last
Whig president and the only nominee of the Know-Nothing party.

The problem now for Fillmore was what to do with the remainder of his life. He was only fifty-six years old and doubted that he
could settle down to a life of retirement. He still did not want to do
anything to bring disgrace to his former position as president, but
was not sure what future lay open to him.

> It is a national disgrace that our Presidents . . . should be cast ad-
> rift, and perhaps be compelled to keep a corner grocery for sub-
> sistence. . . . We elect a man to the Presidency, expect him to be
> honest, to give up a lucrative profession, perhaps, and after we
> have done with him we let him go into seclusion and perhaps
> poverty.

He suggested a $12,000 annual pension for former presidents.

The idea for a pension was more than an abstract idea; the trip
to Europe and other expenses had seriously drained his savings,
and he began to worry tht he would not be able to pay his bills.
Fillmore's financial worries ended in 1858 when he married
Caroline McIntosh, the forty-five year old widow of a wealthy Albany merchant. They purchased a large mansion and began entertaining frequently.

Fillmore took no part in the campaign of 1860, aware that even if he spoke, there was no one to listen. As the Civil War approached, and President James Buchanan hesitated to act, Fillmore joined the rising chorus of critics protesting Buchanan's lack of action. Fillmore said Buchanan should use force to keep the Southern states in the Union arguing that those who sought to leave the Union should be "regarded as an unauthorized assembly of men conspiring to commit treason, and as such liable to be punished like any other unlawful assembly. . . ."

Abraham Lincoln visited Fillmore on February 16, 1861 on his way to his inauguration. The men attended church together and later a benefit to aid Indians. The weekend ended, and neither man ever said what they discussed.

The fighting began, and Fillmore plunged into activities to support the Union. He organized a rally in Buffalo and told the large crowd, "It is no time for any man to shirk from the responsibility which events have cast upon him. We have reached a crisis . . . when no man . . . has a right to stand neutral." He contributed money to the families of Union soldiers, organized a home guard unit, and spoke frequently on behalf of the cause.

He did find much fault with the conduct of the war and at times spoke his mind. During the 1864 presidential campaign, he wrote to a friend that the nation was on the verge of ruin with the prospect of "national bankruptcy and military despotism."

Following his defeat in 1856, Fillmore dedicated his life to public service in his home town. He contributed his time and money to the Buffalo Young Men's Association, supported the library, and was a founder of the Buffalo Historical Society and the Buffalo Fine Arts Academy.

On January 7, 1874, he told friends, "My health is perfect, I eat, drink and sleep as well as ever, and take a deep but silent interest in public affairs, and if Mrs. F's health can be restored, I should feel that I was in the enjoyment of an earthly paradise."

But five weeks later, as he was shaving, he suddenly lost all feeling in his left hand. The paralysis extended to the left side of his face. Two weeks later there was a second stroke and on March 8, he died at the age of seventy-four.

Franklin Pierce

—— twelve ——

The contest for the 1852 Democratic presidential nomination was between James Buchanan and Lewis Cass. Both had strong support, but neither could obtain the two-thirds of the delegates needed for nomination. After 35 ballots, the convention began to cast about for an alternative candidate. Friends of Franklin Pierce, a former senator from New Hampshire, were ready to put forward his name, and he gradually gained strength. On the forty-ninth ballot, he was nominated.

He easily defeated the Whig candidate, Winfield Scott, but his administration was marked by failure. He believed that slavery was protected by the Constitution, and pushed through the pro-slavery Kansas-Nebraska Act of 1854. The new law repealed the Missouri Compromise and allowed Kansas residents to decide if they wanted to be admitted as a slave or free state. It created a civil war within Kansas as pro- and antislavery forces fought bitter battles.

As the convention of 1854 approached, Pierce again wanted his party's nomination. To win, Pierce needed 198 votes, and his managers calculated that he had 145 and the additional 53 votes could be obtained. But he counted too heavily on the support of the South, for which he had done so much. Virginia deserted him, giving its votes to Buchanan on the first ballot. Buchanan held the lead for five ballots, but Pierce was able to remain a close second. On the sixth ballot, Tennessee, another strong Pierce supporter, dropped away and on the seventh ballot Arkansas, Georgia, and Kentucky swung to Buchanan. Pierce's managers knew the cause was lost and withdrew his name, giving the nomination to Buchanan.

That fall, there was a second blow to Pierce, this one from his hometown of Concord. It had been suggested that Pierce visit Concord for a reception in October, but as a committee met to plan the event, a group of Republicans came and packed the meeting. Instead of inviting Pierce, they forced through a resolution saying there would be no reception for the president. He went home in early October to choose a new place to live, and despite the actions of the Republicans, received a rousing reception.

In November, Buchanan won, but Pierce had no bitterness for the man who would take the job he had wanted to keep. Pierce invited Buchanan to stay at the White House before the inauguration.

Outgoing presidents act like homeowners selling their treasured homestead. They occupy their final months with housekeeping details designed to prove that the house was in excellent condition when it was turned over to the new owner. Pierce was no exception. He and his Cabinet prepared endless reports containing thousands of numbers, but no one paid any attention.

It was an emotional departure for Pierce: at his final Cabinet meeting he began to weep, and he spoke with difficulty.

Early in 1853, Pierce announced that he would return to his native New Hampshire and spend the remainder of his life involved in agriculture. On Inauguration Day, Pierce left the White House, but he and his wife stayed in Washington until the weather improved in New Hampshire. He did not have to worry about finances: a frugal man, he had managed to save nearly half of his salary and had a net worth of $78,000.

In late May, Pierce and his wife began their journey home, traveling slowly toward New Hampshire. They spent only a few months at home before leaving for an 18-month tour of Europe.

When he returned in 1859, he found some of his supporters trying to organize a movement to return him to the White House. Pierce had seen Van Buren and Fillmore try to regain the presidency only to be humiliated. He wrote to his supporters telling them he had no intention of returning to active politics. Pierce did have a favorite for the 1860 Democratic presidential nomination: his former secretary of war and close friend, Jefferson Davis. It was an endorsement that would haunt him for the rest of his life.

Then, he was off again, this time to Nassau for a five-month visit. For three years, Pierce had been little more than a vagabond, spending more time in Europe than in the United States, despite his announced plans to spend the rest of his life in Concord. But as the 1860 election approached, Pierce knew the nation was approaching a fateful junction, and he returned home to offer what assistance he could. It would have been better for Pierce if he had stayed away.

His Southern sympathies were a matter of record and even with the threat of Civil War, he continued to make comments favorable to the Southern cause. To a friend he wrote, "No wise man can under existing circumstances dream of coercion." He suggested a compromise; there would be a six-month cooling off period to try to negotiate differences between North and South, but if that failed, then the South could go its own way without interference.

He joined in an ill-fated effort to try to recruit other former presidents to come together to try and find a solution, but once the war came, he became bitter. "To this war . . . which seems to me to contemplate subjugation I give no countenance—no support to any possible extent in any possible war—except thro' inevitable taxation, which seems likely to bankrupt us all."

The extensive traveling had cost Pierce, and the money he had planned to retire on had proven to be inadequate. He began to discuss the possibility of returning to his law practice. But his feelings for the South had seriously damaged his standing.

His denunciations of Lincoln increased as the war went badly for the North, and the Democrats saw a chance to make political gains. He wrote that Lincoln had become a mere tool for the abolitionists "to the extent of his limited ability and narrow intelligence," and was responsible for "all the woe which thus far has been brought upon the Country and for all the degradation, all the atrocity, all the desolution and ruin." But his remarks went beyond politics and to his Northern neighbors they seemed like treason and his friends began to turn away.

On July 4, 1863, Pierce was asked to be the principal speaker at a Democratic rally in Concord. Again he attacked Lincoln for conducting a "fearful, fruitless, fatal civil war . . . it cannot fail to be fruitless in everything except the harvest of woe which it is ripening. . . ."

But as Pierce spoke, a murmur began in the audience, building slowly from the back of the crowd, then spreading quickly. The Union had won a glorious victory at Gettysburg, according to the telegrams arriving at the *Concord Statesman.* Just as Pierce spoke of the hopelessness of war, the Union was winning its greatest battle. On that day, whatever respect Pierce had left in the North evaporated.

Five months later, Mrs. Pierce died, ending an unhappy life marked by frequent melancholy and poor health. He was alone now, and as the war ended, life became almost unbearable. The soldiers returned home but the bitterness against Pierce continued. Almost friendless, Pierce began drinking heavily, often sitting alone in his house consuming bottle after bottle. He spent less and less time in Concord, where few would even talk with him. He had purchased 84 acres along the New Hampshire coast and hit upon a scheme to develop the land as a summer colony, but nothing came of it.

Finally, in 1868, the drinking began to seriously affect his health. Just before dawn on October 8, 1869, he died. The feelings against Pierce were so great in New Hampshire that it took 50 years for the legislature to vote money for a simple monument to the former president.

James Buchanan

—— thirteen ——

James Buchanan was the last in the line of faceless men who ruled the nation between the administrations of Andrew Jackson and Abraham Lincoln. Chosen not for their ability but for their lack of political enemies, they were unable to stop the steady march toward Civil War.

Buchanan, despite four decades of public service, won the 1856 Democratic nomination not for what he had done, but for what he had not done. During much of the Pierce Administration, Buchanan was in London, serving as minister to England. He had avoided the political infighting that claimed better known candidates and emerged as the compromise choice.

His administration was marked with little distinction, and he made it clear he would not accept a second nomination. There was a brief attempt to draft Buchanan, primarily as a holding action by other candidates who thought their chances of winning the nomination would improve with Buchanan in the race, but he would have none of it. To a friend, he said, "I am now in my sixty-ninth year and am heartily tired of my position as President."

In the end, the Democrats split and gave the election to Abraham Lincoln and speeded up the move toward Civil War. South Carolina moved to leave the Union, and other states followed. Buchanan's situation was miserable: he was a lame duck with only four months remaining in his term. His cabinet, peppered with Southerners who would soon play roles in the Confederate government, was of little aid. His hope was to keep the nation together until Lincoln could take over and assume responsibility. Buchanan opposed disunion, but seemed unsure of how to avoid it. He said the government would continue to enforce the laws in all states but added that the government could not coerce a seceding state back into the Union.

Next came a season of compromises. For every problem, a compromise was offered, but all fell short. War was coming, and Buchanan had no idea how to stop it.

On Inauguration Day, Buchanan and Lincoln rode together to the Capitol, chatting almost the entire time. At one point, Buchanan said to Lincoln, "My dear sir, if you are as happy in entering the White House as I shall feel on returning to Wheatland, you are a happy man indeed."

His term over, Buchanan remained in Washington to hold two more meetings with his cabinet. Buchanan felt he and his Cabinet should advise Lincoln on the events at Fort Sumter, even though Lincoln had not asked for advice. The report from the meetings was sent to Lincoln, but there is no indication he ever acknowledged it.

Buchanan returned to his estate in Pennsylvania, receiving an enthusiastic welcome in Baltimore and York, Pennsylvania, along the route. In his hometown of Lancaster, the church bells rang, and the bands played to mark his return. He told the crowd, "I have no language to express the feelings which swell in my heart . . . but I do most cordially thank you for this demonstration of your personal kindness to an old man. . . . I have come to lay my bones among you."

His first month of retirement was exactly as he envisioned it. A wealthy man, who had never married, Buchanan spent his time stocking his home with food and wine and entertaining friends. In the evenings, musical groups came to serenade him.

But the tranquility would not last. On April 12, 1861, the Confederates fired on Fort Sumter. Buchanan wrote to his nephew, "The Confederate States have deliberately commenced the civil war, & God knows where it may end."

Buchanan went into Lancaster frequently to keep up with the latest war news, and with each visit the former president encountered increased hostility. At home, the mail brought what Buchanan called, "violent, insulting and threatening letters." His housekeeper found notes warning that his home would be burned down, and the local Masonic Lodge agreed to provide security. Buchanan was blamed for failing to halt the rebellion before it got started. Republican newspapers picked up the cry against Buchanan. There were implications that Buchanan had actually aided the South by sending extra guns to armories in the Southern states.

Even Lincoln seemed to join the criticism of Buchanan when he said that the "Navy was scattered in distant seas, leaving but a very small part of it within immediate reach of the Government." The Union disaster at the battle of First Bull Run shocked the North. Someone must be responsible, and the handy target was Buchanan.

With every Union setback, the criticism of Buchanan increased. On December 15, 1862, Senator Garrett Davis of Kentucky introduced a resolution to censure Buchanan.

> Resolved, That after it had become manifest that an insurrection against the United States was about to break out in several of the Southern States, James Buchanan, then President, from sympathy with the conspirators and their treasonable project, failed to take necessary and proper measures to prevent it; wherefore he should receive the censure and condemnation of the Senate and the American people.

The resolution failed to pass, but Buchanan was upset by the public debate over the resolution. He decided to defend his actions, but his first letter to a newspaper editor brought only more negative reactions, so he decided to keep quiet. He began gathering papers to support his position, clipping newspaper articles critical of his administration and made notes on his side of the story.

Even though the resolution against Buchanan failed, Congress did inflict a minor inconvenience on him, removing his right to send mail without charge. They acted after hearing rumors that he was sending letters to European governments seeking recognition for the Confederacy. Northern newspapers reported that Buchanan was in England selling Confederate bonds, that he was meeting with spies, and that his Pennsylvania estate had become a center for anti-Union activity.

Buchanan received all of the negative stories. "If there is anything disagreeable in it, some person will be sure to send it to me."

"Nobody seems to understand the course pursued by the late administration," he complained. He set about to try and rectify the situation, deciding to publish a book dedicated to defending himself. He finished the book late in 1862, but he decided that publication at that time would be wrong with feelings running so high. His book, entitled *Mr. Buchanan's Administration on the Eve of the Rebellion,* was not published until 1866, after the war had ended, and tempers cooled. The book was greeted largely by indifference; with the war over, Buchanan was no longer a target of hate. The North had won, and they could now blame men like Jefferson Davis for the war.

Despite the criticism, Buchanan was a strong supporter of the Union cause. He wrote to a friend, "The North will sustain the administration almost to a man; and it ought to be sustained at all hazards." He gave money to equip a volunteer company and even spoke well of Lincoln, calling him, "a man of honest heart & true manly feelings."

Politically, Buchanan had moved from center stage, but he was still sought out by candidates for advice. He did not become involved in the campaign of 1864, but privately opposed the nomination of General George McClellan on a peace platform, saying he would certainly lose the election.

During the war he watched his investments carefully, and his fortune continued to grow. Buchanan was meticulous in his bookkeeping, pouring over his journals for hours at a time. When he sold some land for nearly $15,000, he examined the check and said, "You have made a mistake. Your check is ten cents too little." His financial statement of 1866 listed assets of $205,000 in stocks and bonds, $41,190 in personal loans; $46,560 in real estate, and $16,650 owed by members of his family. Buchanan wrote, "Making all reasonable deductions, I am worth $250,000."

With the war over, life returned to normal for Buchanan; he entertained frequently and traveled extensively within the state. He never returned to Washington. Age was beginning to slow him, and he was well aware that most of the men he had once worked with were dead. "I am now in my 76th year, and all the friends and acquaintances of my youth in your vicinity have been gathered to their fathers."

As he approached death, he turned to religion. He applied to join the Presbyterian Church during the war, but for some unrecorded reason, the church rejected his membership. Finally, in 1865, he was accepted.

In May 1868, Buchanan became seriously ill, a result of old age and a cold. Realizing that the end was near, he sent for the executor of his estate to revise his will. On the last day of May, he told the executor, "I have always felt and still feel that I discharged every public duty imposed on me conscientiously. I have no regret for any public act of my life, and history will vindicate my memory."

The following morning, he died at the age of seventy-eight. His will contained provisions for the church and a fund to provide fuel for the poor of Lancaster. His servants received small bequests, and the rest went to his relatives.

Andrew Johnson

fourteen

Andrew Johnson survived the only impeachment vote against a president by a single vote. Johnson, seeking to carry out the policies of Abraham Lincoln in treating the South with fairness, had run headlong into the Radical Republicans who viewed the Confederate states as conquered territories to be punished. He spent his four-year term watching as the Radicals had their way.

Johnson, a former Tennessee senator, was chosen as Lincoln's running mate in 1864 as a gesture of unity. As the nominating conventions of 1868 approached, Johnson was a man without a party. The Republicans wanted no part of him, and although he did receive a few votes at the Democratic convention, he was viewed as a man who had deserted the party. Johnson knew his presidency was coming to an end, and after four years of fighting, he became more relaxed. Johnson began feeding the mice that lived in the White House, leaving some flour out each night. Later, he began leaving some water for them.

When Inauguration Day came, there was a final insult for Johnson; Ulysses Grant refused to ride in the same carriage with Johnson to the Capitol. Grant would not even talk with Johnson. The outgoing president stayed in his office the morning of Grant's inauguration, signing last minute legislation and winding up his affairs. As the time for the inauguration approached, he rose from his desk, shook hands with each member of his Cabinet, and walked out of the White House alone. He turned at the door and said, "God bless you," to his aides and servants and left without seeing Grant.

He went to Baltimore, where thousands turned out to cheer him at a reception. Nearly a month after his term ended, he began his trip home to Tennessee. Along the way, crowds turned out to welcome him. In Lynchburg, Virginia, where residents once threatened to hang Johnson if he ever set foot in their town, the community leaders honored him.

Johnson had not been home since 1861, and he was shocked by the condition of his Greenville home. When the Confederates occupied Greenville, they used the house as a barracks for soldiers and later as a hospital for wounded soldiers. When the Union army captured Greenville, it became a residence for officers and, finally, a brothel for Negro troops. Although the renovation began before Johnson left Washington, it was not complete when he arrived home.

He had accumulated an estate of $100,000, enough to enjoy a comfortable retirement. But at the age of sixty, he had no intention of retiring. "I intend to appropriate the remainder of my life, short as it may be, in the vindication of my character and that of the state." Tennessee was under the control of a carpetbagger government and Johnson dedicated himself to ridding the state of the hated carpetbaggers.

He found life in Greenville too quiet, writing a friend that it was "as lifeless as a graveyard." To another, he wrote, "There is nothing of interest transpiring in Greenville. All is dull and flat, I long to see a return to Spring when I will be set free from this place forever I hope."

He loved the excitement of politics, despite his unhappy ending as president. Just two years after leaving the White House, Johnson was back in politics. An opening for U.S. senator came up, and Johnson sought to return to his former job. Senators were elected by the state legislature and the race was bitter. Grant announced that he would consider it an insult if Johnson were elected, and the Radical Republicans were outspoken in their opposition to the man they had almost removed from the presidency.

Johnson made impassioned speeches, telling one crowd, "I had rather have the vindication of my state by electing me to my old seat in the Senate of the United States than to be monarch of the grandest empire on earth. . . . For this I live and will never die content without it."

For eight ballots, Johnson led the field, coming within one vote of election. But the radicals were determined to stop him and made a deal to support a compromise candidate to deny the seat to Johnson.

Two years later, in 1872, Johnson was back again, this time campaigning as an independent for an at-large seat. Johnson lost, but so did the Radical candidate, which gave him some measure of satisfaction. Once again, he returned to Greenville and the quiet life he had come to hate.

After the election, he was struck by Asiatic cholera, and for a time it seemed he might die. Gradually, his condition improved, although he would always suffer from the effects of the disease.

In 1874, another Senate seat came open, and once again Johnson began to campaign. Even though the legislature would again select the senator, Johnson wanted to demonstrate that he had popular appeal. The crowds were large as he sought not only to campaign for the Senate but to explain his past actions. In Memphis, he told the crowd:

> I would not be worthy to be called a man unless I was ambitious. I am ambitious of acquiring a name in the minds of the people that I have been a faithful representative; that I have stood upon the watchtowers of my country, and defended and vindicated and guarded the rights when they were not in a condition to do it for themselves. . . . I have lived and toiled for the people because I wanted their approbation and esteem; and when the time shall come that my connection is to be severed with the people and all things that are mortal . . . the most pleasant thought that can pass through my mind will be to feel that I occupied a place in the respect and hearts of my countrymen.

The legislature convened in January 1875 to pick a senator, and the balloting lasted several days. At times, it appeared that Johnson could not win. One candidate came within a single vote of winning, but Johnson, recalling the earlier election he lost, said that anyone who comes within one vote and does not win cannot win. He stayed in the race, and finally, after more than fifty ballots, he won.

On March 5, 1875, the Senate convened in special session, and for the first time since 1869, Johnson returned to Washington, the scene of his greatest glories and humiliations. A few minutes past noon, Johnson walked into the Senate chamber as the packed galleries watched his every move. His desk was covered with flowers sent by wellwishers, but he was surrounded by men who had been bitter enemies. As he walked into the chamber, his enemies pretended they did not see him. They suddenly found things to occupy themselves. Senator Theodore Freylinghausen, a Johnson opponent, pretended to be looking for something beneath his desk. Johnson took the oath of office and began to cry.

Now, Johnson had his chance to extract a measure of revenge against Grant. Seven years earlier, Grant had joined with the radicals against Johnson, then had slighted him at the inauguration. Johnson had been down, and Grant was the hero of the moment. Seven years later, the corruption of the Grant Administration had tarnished the general's standing. On March 22, less than three weeks after returning to the Senate, Johnson spoke out on the floor against the corruption and arrogance of the president.

The special session ended, and Johnson returned home to Tennessee. On the train, he saw some friends from the early years and began talking about his political career. "More than a hundred times, I have said to myself, what course may I pursue so that the calm historian will say one hundred years from now, 'He pursued the right course?'"

Arriving at his daughter's home, he ate lunch and went to his room to talk with his granddaughter Lillie about her upcoming marriage. The conversation ended and Lillie was leaving the room when she heard a noise. Johnson had fallen to the floor. A stroke paralyzed his left side, but he would not let his family send for a doctor.

For a day, he lay in bed, frequently talking of the old days, primarily his youth. A second stroke put him into a coma and the family sent for a doctor. It was too late, he died on July 31, 1875, at the age of sixty-six.

Ulysses S. Grant

fifteen

They had not wanted to leave because they had no place to go. Ulysses S. Grant and his wife loved the power and prestige of the White House and thought the American people would be willing to return them for a third term. They were mistaken; the corruption of his eight years in office was catching up with Grant. The House of Representatives passed a resolution urging Grant not to seek a third term. The resolution spoke of the traditions of Washington and said that for Grant to seek a third term would be "unwise, unpatriotic, and fraught with perils to our free institutions." The resolution passed 234 to 18.

Grant, stung by the rebuke, replied, "It may happen in the future history of the country that to change an Executive because he had been eight years in office will prove unfortunate, if not dangerous." Still, Grant said he would not run again.

As his term drew to a close, so did the prestige Grant and his wife loved. On Inauguration Day in 1877, Rutherford Hayes was sworn in as president and returned to the White House to find a luncheon organized by Mrs. Grant. The luncheon dragged on, and some began to wonder if the Grants would ever leave. They remained in Washington for two more weeks, awaiting the birth of their daughter Nellie's baby, then left for Ohio.

On the train, Grant heard his wife crying, and he asked what was the matter. "Oh, Ulys, I feel like a waif." Grant replied, "Is that all? I thought something had happened. You must not forget that I too am a waif."

Grant had spent most of his life in the army or the presidency. His infrequent flings at private enterprise always ended poorly. Now, he was doomed to spend the rest of his life trading on his past glory.

Two months after leaving the White House, Grant and his wife set off on a marathon tour of the world that lasted two years. They were accompanied by the pomp a member of royalty might expect. The first stop was England where crowds turned out at every point to see the hero of the American Civil War. There were dinners with dukes and duchesses, and crowds of ordinary citizens turned out to cheer him. Briefly, they visited their daughter Nellie, who lived in England with her British husband. Queen Victoria received Grant at Windsor Castle for an awkward dinner that mercifully ended early. Throughout their tour, they were constantly surrounded by people; luncheons were followed by receptions that were followed by dinners and then another reception.

From England, it was on to Belgium, then Germany, Switzerland, Italy, and Denmark. Along the way, Grant shook thousands of hands, almost as if he were still campaigning, a candidate without an election trying desperately to hold on to the roar of the crowd even though they could not understand what he was saying. His trip was covered by reporters traveling with him, and every detail appeared in American newspapers.

They returned to England for another triumphant tour, but this time it was the common citizens who welcomed Grant, turning out by the thousands in the industrial towns to cheer him. Their tributes were sincere, at times moving for the man who had come from humble beginnings like them.

Then, it was on to Paris and Naples, the months passing, but the Grants giving no thought to going home. They spent Christmas of 1877 on a ship off the Italian coast. To start the new year, they went to Egypt, traveling up the Nile to see the Pyramids before moving on to the Holy Land. Then they went to Turkey, Greece, and on to Rome for a call on Pope Leo XIII and dinner with Italian King Humbert. The year sped by as they toured Norway, Denmark, and Russia, where they were received by Czar Alexander II. They visited Otto von Bismark in Berlin.

From time to time, questions were raised in the newspapers about who was paying the bills for all of this. Newspapers unfriendly to Grant speculated that the money came from the U.S.

government or from payoffs while he was in office. The U.S. government did provide Grant with some sea transportation during his trip, and the New York *Herald* paid some bills, but the rest of the money came from Grant.

In India, he received a welcome from the viceroy, Lord Lytton, who held a dinner for Grant and later wrote:

> On this occasion 'our distinguished guest' the double Ex-President of the 'Great Western Republic,' who got as drunk as a fiddle, showed that he could also be profligate as a lord. He fumbled Mrs. A., kissed the shrieking Miss B.—pinched the plump Mrs. C. black and blue—and ran at Miss D. with intent to ravish her. Finally, after throwing all the . . . female guests into hysterics by generally behaving like a musk elephant, the noble beast was captured by main force and carried . . . by six sailors . . . which relieved India of his distinguished presence. . . .

There is little doubt that Lord Lytton exaggerated a great deal in his letter. That Grant would have done those things in front of Mrs. Grant, or that she would have permitted it, is doubtful. However, there is almost certainly some truth in Lytton's letter.

The Grants left India and traveled through the Far East and Siam, then Saigon and China. In Japan, the emperor greeted Grant, shaking his hand, an unusual breach of Japanese tradition.

They had run out of countries to visit and it was time to go home, although Grant would have liked to travel forever. To a friend he wrote, "I am both homesick and dread going home. I have no home but must establish one when I get back; I do not know where."

They arrived in San Francisco, receiving a rousing welcome, and set off on another tour, this time of the United States. Finally, on December 16, 1879, they arrived back in Philadelphia, 31 months after they had left that city. There was a four-hour parade to honor them.

The overseas trip had a number of purposes. First, Grant really had no place to go, and dreaded the thought of returning to his small hometown in Illinois. But more important was the fact that the overseas trip would keep his name in the headlines while keeping him out of domestic political squabbles. Grant wanted desperately to return to the White House, to do what no man had done before, serve a third term as president. Grant maintained that, "I am not a candidate for any office, nor would I hold one that required any maneuvering or sacrifice to obtain," and yet at every stop on his cross-country journey, he met with political leaders.

In truth, he should have stayed away longer: by coming home, he became little more than just another political candidate traveling the country looking for votes. There was no reason for Grant to seek a third term. He had no platform or plan; he needed a job. Finally, he returned to Galena, Illinois, shortly before the Republican convention in Chicago.

On the first ballot, Grant led with 307 votes to 284 for James G. Blaine with the other candidates trailing far behind and 370 votes needed to win the nomination. For days the ballotting went on, candidates gaining and losing a few votes, but none able to capture the prize. Grant drafted a letter of withdrawal and gave it to his floor manager to be used if the cause seemed lost. It was his wife, Julia, who pressed him on, growing furious when she learned of the withdrawal letter and telling his managers that "he must not withdraw his name—no never." In the middle of the convention, Grant was scheduled to pass through Chicago on his way to a speaking engagement in Milwaukee. Julia urged him to speak to the convention, confident that his presence would ignite a stampede for his candidacy, but Grant refused.

It became clear to the delegates that neither Grant nor Blaine could ever win the nomination; the battle lines were too clearly drawn. In the end, the nomination went to a dark horse, James Garfield of Ohio. In a letter to his daughter, Nellie, Grant wrote, "I feel no disappointment at the result of the Chicago Convention. In fact I felt much relieved. The most unscrupulous means had been resorted to by the friends of the other candidates. . . ."

But he was actually bitter and disappointed by the failure. "My friends have not been honest with me. I can't afford to be defeated. They should not have placed me in nomination unless they felt perfectly sure of my success." He campaigned for Garfield, but once Garfield was elected, the new president ignored most of the advice offered by Grant. Gradually, Grant became a critic of Garfield, at one point saying that Garfield did not have the "backbone of an angle worm."

Grant now needed a job and found one as president of the Mexican Southern Railroad, one of the hundreds of small lines that sprang up in the United States and Mexico. In truth, there was no railroad, only a scheme to build a railroad from Mexico City to Oaxaca in the South and to the Rio Grande in the United States.

Grant's role was to be the front man to raise the money necessary to build the line. Grant's need for money was desperate. Following the Civil War, he had received money from grateful citizens, and the interest on this amounted to six thousand dollars a year, a good amount in 1880, but far less than what a man like Grant needed to maintain his lifestyle. He moved to New York, the headquarters for the new railroad. Once again, friends came to his rescue, putting up enough money to buy him a home. For everything, Grant depended upon the charity of others.

Like many things in Grant's life, the railroad turned out to be an illusion. Some money was raised, but it went for Grant's salary and office expenses. There was some minor work on the line, but gradually, in 1884 it slid into bankruptcy. The big money Grant had hoped to reap once again eluded him.

Grant decided to go into business with his son, Buck, who had married well and received one hundred thousand dollars from his father-in-law to go into business with Wall Street broker, Ferdinand Ward. His son offered him a position in the firm of Grant & Ward, with Ulysses S. Grant investing one hundred thousand dollars.

The firm had a bright future, and it seemed to be a good investment, but once again, it turned out to be an illusion. This time, the problem was with Ward, who used the firm's stocks as collateral for more than one loan. This type of fraud works if everything is going well, and the loans are repaid. But things did not go well and on May 4, 1884, things came to a head. Ward told Ulysses S. Grant that he would not be able to cover the loans due the following day.

Grant was desperate and again had to turn to a wealthy friend to bail him out. He went to William Vanderbilt and begged for $150,000 to help the firm out. Vanderbilt said yes, giving Grant a personal loan. But it was not enough; word spread quickly that the firm was in trouble, and Ward fled the country. An investigation showed that instead of having $27 million in assets, there was actually just $67,174. Ward had kept two sets of books, and the real set showed that instead of having $660,000 in the bank, the account was actually overdrawn $2,000,000. A second partner, James Fish, went to prison, and although there were some who thought Grant should also be charged, he escaped prosecution.

Ulysses S. Grant was broke, even destitute, the man who had won the Civil War and served two terms as president, was unable to make a living. His wealthy friends had given him handouts through the years, but none was willing to give him a job. The money he received after the Civil War was invested in second mortgages for railway bonds, but when the bonds stopped paying interest, Grant was left with less than one hundred dollars in cash. President Chester A. Arthur proposed a pension for Grant, but the former president urged that the plan be killed. He did not resist a bill which restored his army rank with a salary of $13,500.

Almost from the moment the Civil War ended, Grant had received offers to write about the war, but he had rejected them all. Now, he needed the money and agreed to write an article for *Century* magazine. The first article appeared in 1885 on the Battle of Shiloh, later in the year a second article on Vicksburg appeared. The two articles paid him a total of $1,000, not nearly enough to live on and repay the $150,000 to Vanderbilt.

In the summer of 1884 he settled in at Long Branch, New Jersey to begin writing a book. He was sixty-two years old, and the cancer that would eventually kill him was beginning to infect his body. His throat was bothering him, starting as a minor pain and growing worse. In the fall, he went to a series of doctors, but the delay in diagnosing the cancer was costly. The growth on his throat had grown dramatically and there was no hope; had it been found just three months earlier, it is probable that surgery would have saved his life.

Grant now faced not only the prospect of dying, but of leaving his widow in desperate financial straights. To ensure that his wife would not become an object of public charity as he had, he worked harder on his book, racing against the cancer that was slowly killing him.

He settled down in his New York home and went to work. Samuel Clements, writing under the pen name, Mark Twain, was one of the nation's most successful writers and a man who admired Grant. Clements wanted to publish Grant's book, offering him an unheard of 30 percent royalty, nearly three times the traditional payment.

In November, he wrote to his daughter Nellie a depressing letter about the state of his health. "I am still very lame and otherwise suffering. I have had a sore throat now for more than four months, and lately I have been suffering from neuralgia. Last Friday I had three large double teeth pulled which I hope will cure the neuralgia. . . ."

In January 1885 Grant's finances improved when Vanderbilt agreed to forgive the $150,000 loan. In March, his doctors feared that death was near, but Grant rallied.

Before he died, Grant would once again be used, this time by real estate promoters of a resort named Balmoral near Saratoga Springs. The owners thought if they could lure Grant to the resort it would dramatically increase their business: if he should die there it might become a national monument. Grant agreed to spend the summer there, becoming a tourist attraction as swarms of visitors came to view the famous general for the final time.

He finished the first volume in June and sent it to the publisher. He read the proofs, making corrections and changes while working to complete the second volume. Finally, he finished the second volume, although he kept insisting that there was more work to be done, more changes and additions. With the end of the book came the end of his reason for living. He wrote to his doctor, "There is nothing more I should do to it now, and therefore I am not likely to be more ready to go than at this moment." Later in July, he wrote, "I do not sleep though I sometimes doze a little. If up I am talked to and in my efforts to answer cause pain. The fact is I think I am a verb instead of a personal pronoun. A verb is anything that signified to be; to do; or to suffer. I signify all three."

At eight o'clock on the morning of July 23, 1885, Grant died.

Following his death, Grant achieved the goal that had eluded him in life, wealth. The two volumes sold an estimated 300,000 at $5 a set. Julia Grant received between $420,000 and $450,000. Mrs. Grant survived for 17 years, moving back to Washington and writing her own autobiography, but it was not published until 1975. She lived to see the beginning of the new century, dying in 1902.

Rutherford Hayes

—— sixteen ——

As a candidate for the presidency in 1876, the primary appeal of Republican, Rutherford Hayes, was his clean record as governor of Ohio and a congressman. After eight years of the corrupt Grant Administration, the Republicans knew that to hold the White House they would have to nominate a candidate above suspicion. The Democrats nominated Samuel Tilden and had high hopes of winning back the White House for the first time since 1856.

Tilden did in fact win the popular and electoral vote, but the electoral vote was close enough to leave the Republicans with some hope. By rigging the electoral vote in Florida and Louisiana, they produced a one vote majority for Hayes but forever removed his image as a politician with a spotless record. His administration was clouded by the fraud, and Hayes produced four years of insignificant accomplishments.

After his nomination, Hayes said it was his "inflexible purpose, if elected, not to be a candidate for reelection for a second term." It is doubtful that Hayes could have been renominated, even if he wanted it. His removal of federal troops from the Southern states ended Republican rule in those states and his backing of civil service reform costs his party patronage jobs. Hayes was hurt that his name was rarely mentioned at the 1880 convention and, as a final insult, the party nominated Chester A. Arthur for vice president even though Hayes had removed Arthur as collector of the port of New York.

Hayes seemed to enjoy the social life of a president but not the pressures that went with it. In 1879, he wrote in his diary, "Lucy and I have had a few minutes' talk on this laborious, anxious, slavish life. It had many attractions and enjoyments, but she agrees so heartily with me as I say: 'Well, I am heartily tired of this life of bondage, responsibility, and toil. I wish it was at an end. . . .'"

Hayes, seeing what had happened to Grant, seemed frightened that his administration would be overtaken by scandal. "We have on the whole enjoyed our four years here. But the responsibilities, the embarrassments, the heartbreaking sufferings which we can't relieve, the ever present danger of scandals and crime among those we are compelled to trust, and a thousand other drawbacks. . . ."

His party kept power with the election of James Garfield, and Hayes looked forward to retirement. "My closing days are full of satisfaction," he wrote in his diary. To a friend he wrote, "Nobody ever left the Presidency with less regret, less disappointment, fewer heartburnings, or more general content with the result of his term (in his own heart, I mean) than I do."

The day after the inauguration, Hayes and his wife boarded a train for the return to Fremont, Ohio where he planned a quiet retirement, with no thought of reentering politics. "We wish to get as completely back into private life as we can; to keep out of public observation enough to show the truth that we have no hankering after the pleasures we have left," he wrote a friend six weeks after leaving the White House.

Almost immediately he encountered financial difficulties. In May 1881 he complained of being land poor. His holdings in Ohio, West Virginia, Minnesota, and North Dakota were worth nearly $300,000, but they were expensive to maintain. He owned stock in the Harvester Company, but when it went bankrupt he was forced to borrow money. Like other presidents before him, he also was responsible for the notes of friends. The financial worries were to continue until his death. Eight months before he died, he wrote in his diary, "Debts large and increasing. I have said yes to appeals too often during the last ten years. The interest on my debt now exceeds my income."

The remaining dozen years of his life after leaving the White House was spent quietly in volunteer work. He contributed both time and money to the Birchard Library and founded the Fremont Board of Trade to draw industry to the small community.

Ironically, he continued to refuse to join a church but became very active in religious work. He was vice-president of the local

Bible Society and became a trustee of his wife Lucy's Methodist church. He contributed a fourth of the cost of building a new church and when it burned down several years later he repeated the offer.

As president, he had been named a trustee of the Peabody Education Fund, dedicated to improving schools in the South. He continued as a trustee after leaving the White House and became more active in the organization. In 1882, he became the first president of a fund to aid Black education in the South. The accomplishments of his years out of politics were probably more significant than his contributions in office. As president of the Slater Fund, he used his influence to obtain a scholarship for W.E.B. DuBois, one of the first civil rights leaders and a founder of the National Association for the Advancement of Colored People.

He served as a trustee of Western Reserve University, Ohio Wesleyan University, and Ohio State University. In each case, he was much more than an honorary member, involving himself in the business of the schools and working to improve their academic programs.

He became an early champion of vocational education, even sending his son, Scott, to a manual-training school, although the boy never used the training he received and later went to Cornell. "I preach the gospel of work, I believe in skilled labor as part of education," he said.

His involvement in public service took him into a relatively new area, prison reform. In 1883, Hayes became president of the National Prison Association, which despite its impressive name was really a small group of reformers attempting to help rehabilitate prisoners. Some questioned why Harrison would become involved with a group that could add little to his prestige. "We prefer to give special attention to the unpopular questions, to those that need friends," he said. He combined his support for manual education with prison reform, urging that inmates be taught a skill to reduce their need to turn to crime.

In 1889, while Hayes was visiting in New York, his wife suffered a stroke, losing her ability to speak. When Harrison returned to Ohio, he found her condition growing worse as she slipped into a coma. Three days after Harrison returned, she died without saying a word. Harrison said, "She is in heaven. She is where all the best of earth have gone." For the rest of his life, thoughts of his wife were never far from his thoughts. He frequently told friends, "I think of Lucy as the Golden Rule incarnate."

For a conservative Republican, his work on behalf of causes including prison reform and Black education was considered to be radical. But Hayes was slowly becoming even more radical. He became involved in organizations concerned with Indian rights and very slowly began to speak out against businessmen who amassed large fortunes while most people lived in poverty.

In 1886, he spoke in Toledo and said, "Free government cannot long endure if property is largely in a few hands and large masses of people are unable to earn homes, education, and support in old age." He turned to reading books and papers about the plight of the poor and advocated changes in the laws regulating corporations and placing a limit on inheritances.

He wrote in his diary that "We ought not to allow a permanent aristocracy of inherited wealth to grow up in our country." He thought that inheritances should be limited to $500,000, with the remainder going to the federal government. In 1888, he wrote, "Vast accumulations of wealth in a few hands are hostile to labor. Their tendency is to break down fair competition, to build up monopoly, to corrupt politics, to bribe conventions, legislative bodies, courts and juries, to debauch society; and churches are not beyond the reach of their baneful influence."

These were strong words from a man whose political success had been financed by the very men he now criticized. He said the United States was becoming "a government of the rich, by the rich, and for the rich." He was speaking out more and becoming more outspoken.

He agreed to address the National Prison Congress which even Hayes admitted was "a little communistic in its tendency."

Hayes, a founder of the original Republican Party, reflected views that would surface in the next century from men like Theodore Roosevelt, Robert LaFollette, and George Norris. But his progressive attitudes had no impact on either his party or his nation.

In 1890, Hayes kept up his hectic schedule, despite the fact that he was now sixty-eight years old. He traveled throughout the country to attend meetings of the many committees he served on. In November 1891, Hayes began a tour of the South to inspect conditions in Southern schools.

By 1893, his mind was clearly on death. He drove a sleigh to visit Lucy's grave and wrote, "My feeling was one of longing to be quietly resting in a grave by her side."

The next day, January 9, Hayes went to Columbus for a meeting of the Ohio State University board and from there went to Cleveland. As he was preparing to leave Cleveland to return home, he suffered a severe pain in his chest. A friend suggested that he remain in Cleveland, but he said, "I would rather die at Spiegel Grove than to live anywhere else." With that he boarded a trail for Fremont and his home at Spiegel Grove.

When he arrived, he was put in bed, and although he talked bravely of trips he planned to make in the future, the end was near. On January 17, 1893, he died after saying, "I know I am going where Lucy is."

Chester Alan Arthur

—— seventeen ——

Of all the men to serve as president, none had a less impressive background than Chester Arthur. A former ward heeler in the New York political machine, Arthur had advanced within the organization to become one of its top lieutenants. As a reward, he was named collector of the Port of New York, one of the top federal patronage jobs, but was removed by President Rutherford B. Hayes in a purge of political appointees.

In the 1880 Republican national convention, Arthur and the New York machine backed Ulysses S. Grant for a third term, but when the nomination went to James Garfield, they needed to throw a bone to the New York machine. The bone was the vice-presidency for Arthur.

When Garfield was assassinated, Arthur became president. If his cronies in the New York machine were expecting a bonanza from their former ally, they were disappointed. Arthur pressed for civil service reform and signed the first comprehensive civil service reform legislation. He worked for federal aid to schools, urged Congress to appropriate money to eliminate illiteracy, and vetoed a bill that would have stopped Chinese immigration.

As the Republican convention of 1884 approached, Arthur had two obstacles. His civil service reform had improved the quality of government, but in doing so, he had eliminated thousands of patronage jobs controlled by politicians, and it was the politicians who would nominate a candidate.

The second problem was Arthur's failing health. His kidneys were slowly failing; he had high blood pressure and heart disease.

When his illness became so serious that he could not work, the White House issued statements saying he was suffering from a cold.

Arthur knew he was slowly dying, but to let the world know of his condition would have all but ended his influence as president. He wrote to a friend that while he desperately wanted the nomination he would make no personal effort to get it. As the convention approached, polls showed that he was a poor second choice behind James Blaine. In the North, his support was almost nonexistent and in the South his backing came from the political appointees who depended upon Arthur for their jobs.

There was no way for Arthur to be nominated, but he feared that if he withdrew there would be speculation about his health. He could not win, and he would not withdraw. Arthur asked his closest aides to stay away from the convention, but still a number of his supporters continued to work for his nomination.

Frank Conger, an Arthur appointee, was to be an Arthur delegate to the convention and had started to organize other delegates. Arthur called him to the White House and told him bluntly, "I do not want to be re-elected, go to your friends and get them to stop their activities."

The Arthur campaign was so disorganized that when it came time to place his name into nomination at the Chicago convention, his managers had forgotten to line up a nominator. An elderly district attorney from Troy, New York, was quickly pressed into service, but his speech lacked preparation and was poorly received.

On the first ballot, Blaine led with 334½ votes to 278 for Arthur, with half a dozen other candidates dividing the remainder. More than half of Arthur's votes had come from the South, which would not help the Republicans in the general election.

On the second and third ballot, Blaine gained strength, while Arthur lost votes. On the fourth ballot it was all over, and Blaine had won the nomination.

After the convention was over, Conger again visited Arthur, who told him he was suffering from Bright's disease and did not expect to live more than a year or two at best. Arthur said that was the reason he had asked Conger not to campaign on his behalf.

In November, Blaine lost and Grover Cleveland and the Democrats reclaimed the White House for the first time in 24 years. Arthur may have secretly preferred Cleveland to Blaine. Cleveland

and Arthur got along well, and Arthur even attended Cleveland's inaugural ball.

He remained in Washington for several days after his term ended, then left for New York City. He planned to return to the practice of law, but his health had deteriorated too much for him to take an active role in a law firm.

Instead, he was retained by a prestigious firm, given a suite of offices, $1,000 a month and very little to do. He made few public appearances and was frequently too ill to leave his home. He became president of the New York Arcade Railway Company, the forerunner to the city subway system, but it was largely an honorary post.

Eleven months after he left the White House, his condition became even worse. He could consume only milk and pepsin. After that there were a series of close calls as Arthur clung to life but prepared for death. He wrote his will and on November 16, 1885, called his son, Alan, and a friend to his house to take care of some unfinished business. He had the two place thousands of personal and official papers in three large garbage cans and burn the contents in the fireplace. The garbage cans were filled and refilled.

The last of the papers were destroyed late in the evening and Arthur's work was finished: the papers which revealed the workings of the New York political machine were gone. The following morning at eight, his nurse found him unconscious after suffering a massive hemmorhage. He survived for 21 hours then died peacefully.

George Washington supervises work at his Mount Vernon plantation. (Courtesy of Library of Congress)

Picture of Andrew Jackson, taken shortly before his death. (Courtesy of Library of Congress)

Ulysses S. Grant sits on the front step of the home he was staying in shortly before his death. (Courtesy of Library of Congress)

Col. Theodore Roosevelt on the S.S. Arden, returning from South America. (Courtesy of Library of Congress)

Theodore Roosevelt is shown in Africa with an elephant killed on his safari. (Courtesy of Library of Congress)

Chief Justice Taft leaves for vacation, June 12, 1929. (photo by Underwood and Underwood, and Courtesy of Library of Congress)

A crowd gathers outside the Washington home of Woodrow Wilson on Armistice Day. (Courtesy of Library of Congress)

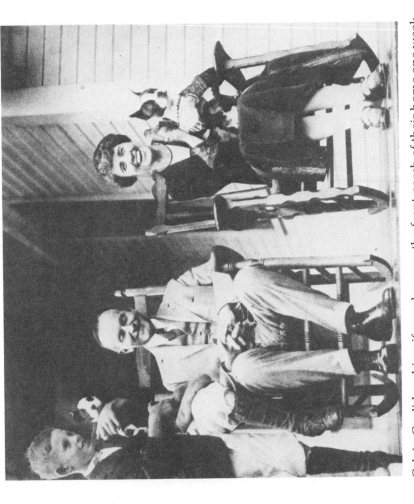

Calvin Coolidge, his wife, and son on the front porch of their home one week after his term ended. (Courtesy of Library of Congress)

Calvin Coolidge fishes in Mill Pond in Pocasset, Massachusetts. He caught nine trout. July 12, 1929. (Courtesy of AP/Wide World Photos)

Herbert Hoover inspects the damage of European nations following World War II. (Courtesy of Library of Congress)

Herbert Hoover shows off one of the five sailfish he caught in Florida just six weeks before the end of his term in 1933. (Courtesy of AP/Wide World Photos)

Herbert Hoover goes fishing on May 29, 1940. "It was a perfect afternoon," said Hoover. (Courtesy of AP/Wide World Photos)

Harry Truman goes for one of his morning walks in Washington on his eightieth birthday in 1964. (Courtesy of AP/Wide World Photos)

Dwight Eisenhower is bird hunting in Albany, Georgia, in 1961. He caught the limit. (Courtesy of AP/Wide World Photos)

Dwight Eisenhower plays golf at Ardmore, Pennsylvania in a charity event in 1964. (Courtesy of AP/Wide World Photos)

Former president Lyndon B. Johnson, clad in a hunting jacket and sports shirt, appears in a happy mood as he chats with newsmen on the front lawn of the LBJ Ranch at Stonewall, Texas in 1969.

Lyndon Johnson talks with Dallas Cowboy Coach Tom Landry after Dallas won the NFC championship in 1972. (Courtesy of AP/Wide World Photos)

Ready for a whirl on Dumbo, the Flying Elephant are former president Richard Nixon and daughter Tricia Nixon Cox during a May, 1982 family visit to the Walt Disney World vacation kingdom. Mrs. Nixon and family friend Bebe Rebozo also prepare for a ride aboard the Fantasyland attraction. © Walt Disney Productions.

Former president Nixon is accompanied by his aide, Col. Jack Brennan, as he golfs at the Shore Cliffs course near his San Clemente, California, home in 1977. (Courtesy of AP/Wide World Photos)

Gerald Ford plays tennis in Houston to raise money for James Baker in 1978. (Courtesy of AP/Wide World Photos)

Gerald Ford skis near his home in Vail, Colorado, around Christmas, 1977. (Courtesy of AP/Wide World Photos)

Jimmy Carter works on handmade chairs which were later auctioned to raise money for the Carter library in 1983. (Courtesy of AP/Wide World Photos)

Grover Cleveland

—— eighteen ——

Grover Cleveland was the only president to leave the White House twice. He was the first Democrat to be elected president in a quarter century and within a year became the only president to be married in the White House. Cleveland married 26-year-old Frances Folsom, the daughter of his former law partner.

During his first term, he managed to antagonize a number of powerful groups, including the veterans, when he vetoed a measure to give unemployed veterans $12 a month. He was renominated in 1888, but this campaign was much different than the one four years earlier. Not only had he lost the support of a number of groups, but his campaign organization was surprisingly weak for an incumbent.

The crucial difference was the opposition from the New York City Democratic machine. Cleveland polled 100,000 more votes than his Republican opponent, Benjamin Harrison, but lost the electoral vote 233 to 168. Cleveland lost New York by 13,000, which gave the election to Harrison.

He believed he had been a good president and told friends he would not have done anything differently. He told one friend, "You cannot imagine the relief which had come to me with the termination of my official term."

His wife did not want to leave and told a White House servant, "I want to find everything just as it is now when we come back again. You know, we are coming back just four years from now."

As he prepared to leave office, he gave what may have been the most radical speech ever given to Congress by a president.

Cleveland said there was trouble coming in the United States brought on by the widening gap between rich and poor, between employers and their workers. He said workers were being "trampled to death beneath an iron heel." He blamed industrialists for this state of affairs.

He had moved into the White House by himself but now was moving out with a wife. He faced the problem of where to make his new home. He would not go back to Buffalo, the city which had given him his political start as mayor, but where the newspapers and some leading citizens had turned against him in the 1884 campaign when it was revealed that he had fathered an illegitimate child. He wrote to a friend that Buffalo had become "the place I hate, above all others." He decided to settle in New York City, accepting an association with the prestigious law firm of Bangs, Stetson, Tracy and MacVeagh. He was not a full partner but used the firm's offices and resources and picked the cases he wanted. "The best thing to do with ex-Presidents is to leave them alone to earn an honest living like other people," he said.

His four-year interlude between terms were probably the happiest years of his life. He worked as much or as little as he wanted, had plenty of time to spend with his growing family, and was treated as a distinguished elder statesman. He was offered the opportunity to speak, usually for large fees, but chose to stay close to his wife and children and devote more time to his hobby, fishing. He made no effort to remain in the public eye, and yet as the election of 1892 approached, more and more party leaders turned to Cleveland to once again lead the party. The opposition was weak, and Cleveland easily won the 1892 Democratic nomination and a chance for a rematch with Harrison.

In the general election, Cleveland did better than he had in his two previous campaigns. He gained 277 electoral votes to Harrison's 145. But the storm clouds were already forming even before he took office for the second time. The nation was falling into an economic depression, which Cleveland would inherit. Banks and businesses were failing in large numbers; farmers unable to sell their crops lost their farms. It tainted his second term, and when the Democrats held their 1896 convention, the party platform repudiated most of Cleveland's views and nominated William Jennings Bryan. Cleveland took Bryan's nomination as a personal insult.

Cleveland sat out the election, refusing to campaign for Bryan, who lost to William McKinley. Although McKinley was a Republican, his views were closer to Cleveland's than Bryan's. McKinley easily won, and for the second time Cleveland moved from the White House.

Again, he rejected the idea of going back to Buffalo. "My home is no longer home."

He briefly considered returning to New York City, perhaps to join one of the many law firms that made attractive offers, but he no longer had the energy to practice law. He was nearly sixty years old, but eight years as president had left him appearing even older. During his second term he underwent a successful operation for cancer, but he was still weak.

He decided to settle in Princeton, New Jersey, to be near friends. His life there quickly settled into a routine as he wrote magazine articles and prepared speeches to give to a variety of groups. Gradually, his popularity returned, but he never again became involved in politics.

Ironically, he did become involved in a fight with Woodrow Wilson, the president of Princeton University, who was twelve years away from becoming president of the United States. Wilson was trying to institute academic and social reforms at Princeton to make the university more democratic. Cleveland, whose friends included old-line members of the Princeton faculty, opposed the reforms and as a school trustee carried the banner for the traditionalists.

In 1905, he accepted an appointment as a board member of the Equitable Life Assurance Society. The company had come under investigation for various questionable business dealings, and Cleveland was brought aboard to give the company some instant prestige and to help reorganize the firm. Two years later, he was named to head the Association of Presidents of Life Insurance Companies, an organization dedicated to fighting government regulation and interference.

He was worth $300,000 to $350,000 but worried that his wife would have difficulty supporting his five children. In a magazine article, he called for a pension for former presidents. Perhaps because he had been a former president twice, he was frequently asked his views on life after the White House. Jokingly, he referred to a newspaper editor who suggested that former presidents should be taken to a five-acre lot and shot. Cleveland said, "In the first place, a five acre lot seems needlessly large, and in the second place an ex-President has already suffered enough."

The return of his popularity pleased him. When he left the White House in 1897, he told a friend, "I don't know in the shuffle what will become of me and my poor old battered name . . ." Now his name was being restored.

He turned down attractive offers to write his autobiography saying, "What I did is done, and history must judge its value, not I. My private life has been so commonplace that there is nothing to write about."

His health was increasingly precarious and on June 24, 1908, he died quietly in his bed at Princeton at the age of seventy-one. His final words were, "I have tried so hard to do right."

Benjamin Harrison

nineteen

For Benjamin Harrison, the presidency was an undistinguished end to an undistinguished career in politics. He served a single term in the U.S. Senate, and when the Republican National Convention became deadlocked between John Sherman and Walter Q. Gresham in 1888, Harrison was the compromise candidate. Assuming that President Grover Cleveland would be easy to defeat, Harrison conducted his campaign from his home in Indianapolis. Even though Cleveland had lost much of his popularity, Harrison won one of the closest elections, trailing Cleveland in the popular vote, but winning the electoral vote.

He proved to be a weak president, yielding to Congress and pressure groups who demanded higher government spending for pet projects and higher tarriffs.

Despite a challenge from James Blaine, Harrison was able to gain his party's nomination in 1892, but lost the election to Cleveland, the man he had defeated four years earlier.

The loss did not affect Harrison as much as the death of his wife several days before the election. Harrison seemed almost relieved to be leaving the White House, writing to Colonel Fred Grant, the son of Ulysses S. Grant, "I would hasten, if I could, the time when I can surrender all public cares." To another friend he said, "This is my prison. The first question about any man that goes into the White House is whether he is tough enough to live through it."

Harrison attended Cleveland's inauguration then left for Indianapolis where he was greeted by a large, cheering crowd. "I made no mistake in coming home at once, there are no friends like the old ones," Harrison later told his son Russell.

His first task was to repair his house, which he said "needed the labor of almost every known trade to restore the waste of the campaign of 1888 and also of the tenants who have occupied it in my absence." To keep the lawn in order, Harrison had a goat shipped from the White House.

Harrison decided to return to the practice of law but only on his terms. He set a minimum retainer of $500 and told clients he would appear in court only in the most important cases. His clients would be buying the status of being represented by an expresident, but only as an associate counsel. He also accepted an offer from Stanford University to give six lectures for $25,000. The *Ladies Home Journal* offered Harrison $5,000 for a series of nine articles, which were turned into a book entitled, *This Country of Ours*. The book sold well and was translated into five languages. Harrison turned down offers to become president of a bank and professor at the University of Chicago. He wrote to a friend, "I find myself exceedingly lazy, unable yet to do much of any work."

Despite the frequent presence of his children and grandchildren, Harrison found himself becoming increasingly lonely. In 1895, three years after the death of his wife, Harrison proposed to Mary Lord Dimmick, a thirty-nine year-old widow who was his late wife's niece. She had come to know Harrison when she nursed his wife during her final months. His children, Mary and Russell, reacted negatively to the news that their cousin would become their stepmother.

In trying to win over his son, Harrison wrote him, "It is natural that a man's former children should not be pleased ordinarily, with a second marriage. It would not have been possible for me to marry one I did not very highly respect and very warmly love. But my life now, and much more as I grow older, is and will be a very lonely one and I cannot go on as now. A home in life is essential to me and it must be the old home. Neither of my children live here—nor are they likely to do so, and I am sure they will not wish me to live the years that remain to me in solitude."

The engagement was announced near Christmas in 1895, and the couple were married the following April in New York City. It is clear that Harrison deeply loved his new wife. After attending a concert with her, he told a friend, "I am not devoted to music but

Mrs. Harrison is, and I am devoted to her." On February 21, 1897, Mrs. Harrison gave birth to a girl, and she was named Elizabeth after Harrison's mother.

As other presidents have discovered, Harrison found that his popularity increased after he left the White House. Just as Cleveland had come back from defeat to win the 1892 election, Harrison's supporters thought he might recapture the White House for a second time.

Harrison did nothing to encourage the speculation and worked actively to discourage it. He joked to a friend, "Few of the newspaper writers seem to get on to the fact that a poor ass, that is carrying three loads, cannot expect to be as frisky as a lead colt."

He called the talk of another campaign ridiculous and told political leaders, "I do not see anything but labor and worry and distress in another campaign or in another term in the White House." Still the talk would not end and Harrison wrote, "The repugnance to further public service deepens with me every day." To another friend he wrote, "I am not insensible to approval or applause, but I am not very anxious just now to make myself more popular. I am sometimes strongly tempted to do something very unpopular for safety."

As the convention of 1896 approached, Harrison withdrew almost completely from public life to discourage any movement to give him the Republican nomination. He wrote a public letter to the chairman of the Indiana Republican committee, saying he would not be a candidate, and to a supporter he wrote, "Another term at Washington would (be) . . . full of cares and trouble for me, and that only. I have thought that a fresh pilot might steer the ship more satisfactorily than I."

With Harrison out of the race, William McKinley easily won the nomination and the right to face Democrat William Jennings Bryan. To a friend, Harrison wrote, "I am altogether pleased to be out of the political struggle which is now waxing warm. It is a great comfort to have the newspapers turn their attention to somebody else, to say nothing of office-seekers."

He spent the summer at his cabin in the Adirondacks, but politics could not be completely forgotten. McKinley and his campaign manager, Mark Hanna, perhaps overestimating the strength of Bryan, pleaded with Harrison to help the Republican ticket. Finally, Harrison yielded and agreed to campaign in New York, Virginia, West Virginia, and Ohio. McKinley won, but Harrison declined a major position in the administration, accepting instead a minor post as a member of the International Court late in McKinley's term.

Harrison returned to private life, spending as much time as possible with his wife and young daughter. He devoted more time to his law practice, handling a wide range of cases including libel, inheritance taxes, patent law, and railroad cases.

His biggest case came in 1898 when he was hired by Venezuela to represent that nation in a boundary dispute with the British. Venezuela originally sought to hire another former president, Grover Cleveland, but he turned down the case. The South American nation needed an attorney with enough prestige to make an impression before the five-member international court selected to hear the case. Harrison demanded and got top dollar for his services. His retainer was $20,000 plus $10,000 for every 3 months he worked on the case. The fee was large, but the work was extraordinary. In early 1899, he wrote to Jose Andrade, the Venezuelan minister in Washington, "I have given myself so absolutely and so constantly to the case of Venezuela since my employment that I have felt recently as if I was on the verge of a breakdown. For one year now I have taken no rest and have not even had the diversion that would have come from other professional engagements."

The tribunal began hearing the case on June 15, 1899, in Paris before two British, two American, and one Russian judge. Harrison had prepared his case well, overwhelming the British arguments. But the case was decided not on its merits but on politics. The British and Russian judges combined and in the end, Venezuela received only a tenth of the land it claimed. Harrison and his family left Paris shortly after the decision was announced and set off on a brief tour of Europe with his wife and daughter.

Despite the loss, he continued to be in demand, arguing cases before the Indiana Supreme Court and federal appeals courts. But his pace was more leisurely; he decided he would never again become involved in a case that consumed all of his time.

Like Rutherford Hayes, Harrison became more liberal after leaving the White House. He spoke out against big business and monopolies. In Chicago, he spoke on "The Obligations of Wealth." In a later speech, he said, "Monopoly is offensive; it destroys individual enterprise; it antagonizes the principle of personal liberty which is the very cornerstone of Republican government; and is a menace to the people. . . ."

He avoided the Republican convention in 1900, which renominated McKinley, and took a long trip through the Northwest. Although he accepted an appointment on the International Court, his failing health prevented him from ever taking his seat. In early March 1901, he came down with a cold, which turned into pneumonia. He did not respond to medication, and his condition became worse. Mrs. Harrison maintained a constant vigil by his bedside and held him in her arms as he died on March 13 at 4:45 P.M.

His widow survived Harrison by 47 years and died in 1948 in New York.

Theodore Roosevelt

—— twenty ——

Even before the last votes were counted in the 1904 presidential election, the landslide winner, Theodore Roosevelt, made his dramatic announcement: he would not be a candidate for a third term in 1908. Roosevelt had taken office in 1901 after the assassination of William McKinley. At forty-three, he was the youngest man to become president, and it meant that when he left office in 1909 he would be just fifty years old, too young for a man with Roosevelt's energies to retire.

He was able to deliver the 1908 Republican nomination to his candidate, William Howard Taft, and as Taft's inauguration drew near, Roosevelt's sister described him "as gay as a boy let out of school." So close was Roosevelt's friendship with Taft that he invited the Tafts to move into the White House before the inauguration. Roosevelt watched his successor being sworn in then slipped out a side door of the Capitol and headed for the train station where he said, "Good-bye and good luck" to those who came to see him off.

Roosevelt told friends that he wanted no part of politics once his term ended. "When I stop being President I will stop completely," he wrote. However, there were indications that from the day his term ended he missed the presidency. He told William Jennings Bryan, "When you see me quoted in the press as welcoming the rest I will have, take no stock of it. . . . I will confess to you that I like my job. The burdens . . . will be laid aside with a good deal of regret." Once he pointed to his wrist and said, "I would cut my arm off right there if I could recall that written statement" saying he would not be a candidate in 1908.

From the moment he left the White House, there was speculation about what Roosevelt would do next. Some thought he might become president of his alma mater, Harvard. There was also a movement to run him as a candidate for the U.S. Senate from New York, but nothing came of either idea. Instead, Roosevelt took a job as a contributing editor of *The Outlook,* a small magazine with influence beyond its small circulation. He was to be paid $12,000 a year and contribute one article a month on whatever topic he chose. It would leave him with plenty of time to pursue his other duties while giving him an anchor, an office to work from.

Roosevelt quickly grew restless, and like Grant 30 years earlier, he began to plan an extensive foreign trip. It would be an expensive trip, and to underwrite the cost he contracted with Scribner's which agreed to pay him $50,000 for a series of articles on his trip in Africa. But, unlike Grant, Roosevelt sought to make the African trip as private as possible: no reporters would be allowed. However, it is unclear whether Roosevelt sought to protect his privacy or his deal with Scribner's magazine. Even *The Outlook,* which was paying him a salary, was banned from covering his African trip.

The African safari was an adventure for Roosevelt and the catch included lions, rhinoceroses, hyenas, and giraffes. For nearly a year, Roosevelt was all but lost to the world, communicating only through his articles for *Scribner's.* On March 14, 1910, Roosevelt emerged from the African jungle at Khartoum, and reporters raced to meet him. He would only talk off the record, however, getting more information about politics back home than he gave on his trip. He would not talk about politics or the performance of Taft.

In Khartoum he was reunited with his wife, whom he had not seen for a year. Also waiting for him in Khartoum were dozens of invitations from European nations. France wanted him to speak at the Sorbonne, the English offered an honorary degree to Oxford, and the Kaiser invited him to Berlin. Norway and Austria-Hungary followed with invitations.

First there was a stop in Cairo and then Rome where he was received by the Pope. France was a rousing success: his speech was reprinted, and copies sent to every teacher in the country. He stopped briefly in Belgium, Denmark, and the Netherlands. The welcomes were all warm and friendly.

In June 1910, Roosevelt returned to the United States and found the Republican party in turmoil. Taft's popularity had fallen dramatically, and he decided to reach out to Roosevelt for help. He asked the former president to come to the White House to meet with him, hoping to get some advice and thinking that some of Roosevelt's popularity might rub off on him. But Roosevelt would not go, writing to Taft, ". . . I don't think it well for an ex-President to go to the White House, or indeed to go to Washington, except when he cannot help it."

Roosevelt may have been reluctant to meet with Taft, but he showed no reluctance to meet frequently with men who had become disenchanted with Taft. Because Taft held genuinely warm feelings for Roosevelt and considered him one of his best friends, he was slow in seeing trouble coming. He could not accept the fact that Roosevelt, the man who put him in the White House, might have turned against him. Gradually, he realized the truth and told a friend, "I do not see how I am going to get out of having a fight with President Roosevelt." His wife, Nellie, was even more direct, telling her husband, "Well, I suppose you will have to fight Mr. Roosevelt for the nomination, and if you get it he will defeat you. But it can't be helped. If possible you must now allow him to defeat you for the renomination. It does not make much difference about the re-election."

Later that year, in 1910, Taft was surprised to read in the newspapers that Roosevelt planned to visit him at the summer White House in Massachusetts. By this time, Taft did not want to see Roosevelt, saying, "I hope he will not come."

Taft did meet with Roosevelt for the first time since the inauguration sixteen months earlier. The meeting between the two once close friends was stilted, and the two failed to come closer together.

Roosevelt began making speeches, and in August he started off on a 5,500 mile tour through 14 states, reaching as far West as Wyoming. It was clear that Roosevelt was campaigning, but no one, including Roosevelt, knew exactly where it would lead.

There was, of course, the problem of Roosevelt's 1904 statement that he would not run for a third term. As best he could, he tried to explain it away. He said that what he meant was that he would not run for a third consecutive term, but that he might run later, perhaps in 1912, 1916, or 1920.

It was a strange contest: Roosevelt, who badly wanted to return to the White House, to the limelight and the power that went with it, against Taft, who was uncomfortable in the White House and disliked the power. In late February 1912 Roosevelt announced his candidacy, which came as no surprise to anyone.

Taft complained, "If I only knew what the President (Roosevelt) wanted, I would do it, but you know he has held himself so aloof that I am absolutely in the dark. I am deeply wounded, and he gave me no chance to explain my attitude to him."

Roosevelt would be the people's candidate, running against what he said were the politicians who sought power for themselves, politicians opposed to reforms such as direct primaries. In fact, Roosevelt had a good reason to support the direct primaries. Taft controlled the party machinery, which would select most delegates to the Republican convention; Roosevelt might win the few direct primaries but still not win the nomination.

Roosevelt's campaign drew the support of some of the nation's wealthiest men. By comparison, Taft, who supposedly had the support of the old guard, had difficulty raising money and had to turn to his wealthy brother, Charles, to keep his campaign going.

Taft held the South where there were no primaries and the only Republicans owed their jobs to Taft. In the rest of the country, Roosevelt campaigned hard, perhaps harder than any candidate for president. Speech followed speech until in April he lost his voice and was forced to cut back his hectic schedule.

There was a third candidate in the race, Wisconsin senator Robert LaFollette trying desperately to take on the popular expresident and a sitting president. He could not win but he could have an impact. In North Dakota, one of the first primary states, Roosevelt finished second to LaFollette, while Taft was a distant third. In New York, Roosevelt's home state, Taft won an overwhelming majority of the delegates, and Roosevelt cried foul. "They are stealing the primary elections from us . . . ," he said. With the support of the Chicago *Tribune,* Roosevelt won the Illinois primary, and four days later he won an impressive victory in Pennsylvania.

Slowly, both were inching toward the number of delegates needed to win. Increasingly the battle became a personal fight. "I am in this fight to perform a great public duty—the duty of keeping Theodore Roosevelt out of the White House," Taft said. Still, at times he had doubts about running against his old friend and mentor. Campaigning at one point he said, "I am here to reply to an old friend of mine, Theodore Roosevelt, who has made many charges against me. I deny those charges. I deny all of them. I do not want to fight Theodore Roosevelt, but sometimes a man in a corner fights. I am going to fight."

As the Republican convention approached, it was clear that neither man had enough votes to win the nomination. Both were about 75 votes short, and the outcomes centered on delegates who were in dispute. Unfortunately for Roosevelt, Taft controlled the party machinery, which would decide which delegates to seat. The committee voted again and again to seat the Taft delegates, driving Roosevelt to call the voting, "a fraud as vulgar, as brazen, and as cynically open as any ever committed by the Tweed regime. . . ."

When the committee had done its work, 235 of the 254 disputed seats had gone to Taft and with them the nomination. Still, Roosevelt would not give up and decided to go to the convention personally to campaign. His ploy did not work and as he saw his chance for the nomination fade, he began to think about a third party effort. On the convention floor, the Roosevelt supporters were becoming increasingly bitter, and when it came time to select a nominee, most refused to cast their votes. Taft polled 561 votes, just 21 over the majority. Roosevelt had come so close, but already he had made up his mind to form his own party.

The Democrats nominated Woodrow Wilson in a convention that was nearly as bitter as the Republican's, and the battle was on. To his dismay, Roosevelt found that many of the political leaders who had supported him for the nomination now returned to Taft. It was one thing for a Republican to oppose Taft for the nomination, but quite another to leave the party to back Roosevelt.

Both Taft and Roosevelt realized that they could not win. Taft wrote his wife, "Sometimes I think I might as well give up as far as being a candidate is concerned. There are so many people in the country who don't like me." Roosevelt thought he would finish ahead of Taft but when a friend asked him if he could beat Wilson, Roosevelt said, "I think this very improbable."

As he had in the primaries, Roosevelt campaigned hard, while Taft all but gave up and for the most part remained in the White House. On October 14, Roosevelt was campaigning in Milwaukee where he planned to make a major address. As he left his hotel and stepped into the car that would take him to the auditorium, a man stepped from the waiting crowd and, as Roosevelt stood in the car and waved to the crowd, the man pulled an old fashioned pistol and shot Roosevelt in the chest. A Roosevelt aide, Elbert Martin, saw the man before the first shot was fired, and, before the man could fire again, Martin leaped atop him and drove him to the ground. Roosevelt watched the man being forced to the ground and said, "Don't hurt him. Bring him here. I want to look at him."

The man, John F. Schrank, a part-time bartender who was opposed to Roosevelt's seeking a third term, was brought to Roosevelt who asked Schrank why he had shot him. Schrank was taken away by police before he could reply. Schrank was found to be insane and spent the rest of his life in a mental institution.

The wound was not serious: the bullet had struck his coat pocket, passing through a bulky copy of the speech he planned to deliver that night and his metal glasses case, entering his chest where it struck a rib and stopping just short of his right lung.

His aides prepared to take him to the hospital, but Roosevelt would not go: he wanted to deliver his speech. He was taken to the auditorium where he told the crowd, "I don't know whether you fully understand that I have just been shot; but it takes more than that to kill a Bull Moose." He went on to talk about his campaign for nearly an hour. After the speech, he was taken back to Chicago where doctors removed the bullet, finding that his rib had been broken by the bullet. He spent one week in the hospital, then went to his New York home where he rested for another week, and returned to campaigning with a speech at Madison Square Garden.

The election went as Roosevelt thought it would: Wilson won 6,293,019 votes to Roosevelt's 4,119,507 with Taft trailing with 3,484,956. Taft carried just two states, Utah and Vermont.

Roosevelt's comeback had failed. Some leaders in his Progressive Party hoped Roosevelt would now begin thinking about returning to the stage in 1916, but Roosevelt realized that it would be impossible to hold the Progressives together for four more years. They had been able to unite for a brief time behind Roosevelt, but within the Progressive movement were actually dozens of smaller movements all with their own goals. And unlike the Democrats and Republicans, the Progressives had no spoils to distribute to the faithful. To a friend, Roosevelt wrote, "The fight is over. We are beaten. There is only one thing to do and that is to go back to the Republican party."

With his political career seemingly over, Roosevelt turned to writing his autobiography, a tame volume that was overly polite, even to his enemies. During the campaign of 1912, rumors began to circulate that Roosevelt was a heavy drinker, a far cry from the truth. The rumor was widespread, but because no newspaper had printed the story there was no way for Roosevelt to deny it without risking wider distribution. Finally, in the closing days of the campaign, a trade publication in Michigan called *Iron Ore* ran a story saying that Roosevelt "gets drunk, too, and that not infrequently. . . ."

Roosevelt waited until after the campaign was over, and then did what thousands of politicians have wanted to do; he filed a libel suit. Roosevelt won the case, and the publication was forced to print a retraction and at Roosevelt's request pay on minimum damages—six cents, but it was a victory Roosevelt relished.

He still lusted for adventure, and, in 1913, the opportunity for a new adventure came. The governments of Brazil, Chile, and Argentina invited him to speak in their countries. But, of course, Roosevelt could not travel like any ordinary tourist; he decided to travel the South American continent from South to North, moving up the rivers through areas that were uncharted and unseen by white men.

It was the final adventure in a life of excitement, and Roosevelt plunged into the trip. It was grueling, with Roosevelt carrying much of the burden of work. They left New York on October 4, going to Argentina, Uruguay, and Brazil. Roosevelt was accompanied by his son, Kermit, and twenty others. They used dugout canoes for the journey. The trip was harrowing, food was in short supply, and at times there was serious doubt that they would succeed. Kermit nearly drowned after he was thrown from his canoe, and Kermit, Theodore, and most of the party came down with a fever.

Roosevelt badly injured his leg in a canoe accident, developing deep abscesses, which had to be lanced and drained. At one point, Roosevelt felt that he could not go on. "We have reached a point where some of us must stop. I feel I am only a burden to the party," he told Kermit.

The journey was much more dangerous than anyone had imagined, and even Roosevelt admitted, "It was time to get out," and. as quickly as possible they made their way from the interior of South America. Back in New York, it was clear that the trip had taken a serious toll on Roosevelt. One friend said the trip "stole ten years of his life," and his sister said he never was "wholly free from recurrent attacks of the terrible jungle fever." The New York *Times* ran pictures of Roosevelt before and after the South American trip to illustrate how much thinner and older he looked.

Two weeks after his return from South America, he was off again, this time to Spain for the wedding of his son. When he returned to the United States, his doctor examined him and recommended a four-month rest. In addition to his problems with the fever he picked up in South America, his spleen was enlarged.

In 1914, the Progressives tried to convince Roosevelt to run for governor of New York, but Roosevelt declined the offer. It did not mean he was through with politics, but rather that he knew the Progressive party would not be the vehicle to carry him to success.

Just as he had with Taft four years earlier, Roosevelt was becoming troubled by the actions of Wilson's administration. World War I came in 1914, and Roosevelt joined with Wilson in urging neutrality, although in private Roosevelt sided with the English. After several months of public neutrality, Roosevelt came out publicly in favor of the British. The issue was the German invasion of neutral Belgium, and the alleged atrocities committed by the German army in invading the small nation. Increasingly, his writings were critical of Wilson and his foreign policy, calling the Wilson administration "these shivering apostles of the gospel of national abjectness."

For Roosevelt, the problem was that the outcome of his policy would be war, while Wilson cautioned peace. There was little support in the United States for war and therefore few were willing to follow Roosevelt.

In the 1914 campaign he did some minor campaigning for Progressive candidates but clearly had little love for the task. To a friend he wrote, "I believe that my usefulness in public life is about at an end, that the prejudice against me is such that I harm rather than help the cause for which I stand." He said he saw 1914 as his final campaign; he was repaying old debts to politicians who had aided him and after that he would be "an absolutely free man." He said that, "Thereafter I am going to say and do just what I damned please."

The Progressives did poorly in the election, and, as Roosevelt predicted, they began to disintegrate. He was becoming a man without a party and realized that he would have to return to the Republicans, although many Republicans still blamed him for the defeat of 1912 and did not want him back.

But politics would take a back seat to events occurring across the ocean when the Germans sunk the *Lusitania* killing 1,200 people including 128 Americans. Roosevelt reacted angrily, calling the sinking "not merely piracy, but piracy on a vaster scale of murder than old-time pirates ever practiced. . . . It is warfare against innocent men, women and children. . . . It seems inconceivable that we can refrain from taking action in this matter, for we owe it not only to humanity but to our own national self-respect."

Wilson protested the sinking, but it was not enough for Roosevelt who said the United States would "earn as a nation measureless scorn and contempt if we follow the lead of those who exault peace above righteousness."

His animosity against Wilson grew and his thoughts turned to the presidential election of 1916. Although Roosevelt said he hoped the Republicans would not nominate him, he clearly wanted to be president again. There was, of course, the question of how to run. He was still the leader of the Progressive party, although he knew he could not win under its banner. He desperately sought to rejoin the Republicans, but did not want to risk losing his Progressive support.

His plan was to run on both tickets, capturing the Progressive nomination, which he thought would be easy, and then winning the Republican nomination. But the Republicans were not in a forgiving mood. Supreme Court Justice, Charles Evans Hughes, led on the first ballot with 253½ votes while Roosevelt had just 65 and ranked eighth in the balloting.

For the Progressives there was a dilemma: they had held back nominating a candidate until the Republicans acted, hoping the Republicans would nominate Roosevelt first. It became clear to Roosevelt that he could not win the Republican nomination, and the Progressive nomination by itself would be worthless.

After a series of meetings between the Progressives and the Republicans, and between Roosevelt and his backers, Roosevelt came up with the preposterous idea that the Progressives should nominate Henry Cabot Lodge for president. The idea was repulsive to the Progressives, who viewed Lodge as a conservative opposed to most of their principles. Wilson would be a more acceptable candidate to the Progressives than Lodge. Finally, the Progressives nominated Roosevelt, just minutes after the Republicans chose Hughes as their candidate.

Roosevelt had no stomach for opposing Hughes and Wilson and telegraphed the Progressives, "I am very grateful for the honor you confer upon me by nominating me as President. I cannot accept at this time. . . ." He endorsed Hughes, and Roosevelt's political career was over. He campaigned for Hughes, not because he liked the Republican candidate, but because he strongly detested Wilson and would do anything to deny him reelection. By the narrowest of margins, Wilson won the election, and Roosevelt began to look ahead to 1920, deeply regretting his failure to capture the 1916 Republican nomination.

Despite Wilson's best efforts, the United States drifted into war. Roosevelt again saw his chance to repeat his brief heroism of the Spanish-American War: there might be another San Juan Hill in Europe where he could again return to center stage. In 1911, during a dispute with Mexico, Roosevelt had asked Taft for permission to lead a military unit, but there was no need for fighting. Three years later, when the United States fought Mexico, Roosevelt again sought to return to military service, if the war should become serious. In 1916, Roosevelt wrote to Wilson's secretary of war, Newton D. Baker, again seeking permission to fight in Mexico.

But his real thoughts were on Europe; since 1915 he had been considering ways to get involved in the war, even if the United States would not. In his mind, he organized an army unit, deciding who would command what, and how the unit would serve. After Wilson broke diplomatic relations with Germany, but before the war started, Roosevelt wrote to Baker reminding him of his willingness to organize a unit to fight in Europe. Baker, who wanted no part of Roosevelt and his unit, wrote back that, if war came, Congress would have to approve any such unit.

Roosevelt was politically astute enough to know when he was being given the cold shoulder. He turned to the French and British, offering to raise a division of Americans to fight under their flag. He told the French ambassador to the United States, "At this time I think I could do this country most good by dying in a reasonably honorable fashion, at the head of my division in the European War."

On April 2, 1917, war came, and once again Roosevelt lobbied Baker. He again asked for permission to organize a division and said he would raise the money to underwrite the cost until Congress could approve the necessary money. Again Baker said no, only Congress could give Roosevelt authorization to start such a division. Roosevelt tried again and again Baker said no, this time becoming a little patronizing in his reply. "The patriotic spirit of your suggestion is cordially appreciated," Baker wrote.

It was a tragic time for the man who had fought in Cuba two decades before and had served as commander in chief of all the armies as president. On the day Wilson asked Congress to declare war, Roosevelt turned up at the White House, but Wilson said he was too busy to see him. So, Roosevelt, who had spent five years criticizing Wilson, now issued a statement praising him, and mentioning that he was ready to serve if Wilson would let him.

One week later, Roosevelt returned to Washington to again plead for his division. This time he did get to see Wilson, talking for an hour but receiving only evasive answers to his questions about forming a new division. Roosevelt continued his lobbying, enlisting the aid of congressmen and senators, but Baker stalled, telling Roosevelt there were "doubtless other ways in which that value could be contributed apart from a military expedition." Baker thought Roosevelt could help, but not in an active role. Roosevelt kept writing; each letter to Baker was more detailed about his military plans, but each time Baker said no. With each rejection, Roosevelt became increasingly depressed. Finally, even Roosevelt realized that there was no hope; he issued a statement saying he had no choice but to "disband and abandon all further effort. . . ."

His four sons did join the war effort, leaving Roosevelt almost alone at Oyster Bay. For the first time in his life, there was nothing to look forward to; at the age of fifty-eight it appeared that both his political and military careers were over.

But political careers do not die quickly, even when the candidate is humiliated; there is always hope that in another year, with another issue, things might be different. As 1920 approached, Roosevelt thought events might be coming his way. He told his sister Corrine, "I have only one fight left in me, and I think I should reserve my strength in case I am needed in 1920." To a friend he said, "If the Republican party wants me . . . I will be a candidate."

In 1918, he hit the campaign trail again, working to elect Republican congressional candidates. He kept in constant touch with his four sons serving in the army. Theodore, Jr. and Archie both suffered serious wounds, although both recovered. On July 17, came the terrible news that his son, Quentin, a flyer, was shot down behind enemy lines and killed. He was not yet twenty-one, the youngest of the Roosevelt boys, and Roosevelt wrote, "It is a very sad thing to see the young die, when the old who are doing nothing, as I am doing nothing, are left alive."

The fall election went the Republican's way: they gained control of both the Senate and the House. Roosevelt's position was strengthened by the results, but the death of his son had left a void, and now he wondered if even the presidency could fill it. His health continued to cause problems: the fever he contracted in South America reappeared from time to time, and he had the added burden of rheumatism. He was in and out of the hospital, and each time his condition seemed to deteriorate.

He returned home for Christmas in 1918, but by now his family realized that his health was fragile indeed. The new year came, and on Sunday, January 5, 1919, Roosevelt did not leave his room, staying in bed while his wife Edith read to him. At 11 o'clock he asked his valet to turn down the small lamp, "Will you please put out the light."

The valet settled into a nearby chair and watched as Roosevelt fell asleep. At 4 A.M., the valet was awakened by Roosevelt's irregular breathing pattern, and he went to get help. He returned with a nurse, but Roosevelt's breathing had stopped. They called Mrs. Roosevelt, who leaned over Roosevelt's body and said, "Theodore, darling." There was no answer. The cause of death was a pulmonary embolism, a blood clot in his lungs. He was sixty years old when he died.

William Howard Taft

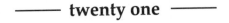

—— twenty one ——

Of all the presidents, only William Howard Taft achieved his greatest success after leaving the White House. He had never really wanted to be president but was pushed forward by his ambitious wife, Nellie, and his political mentor, Teddy Roosevelt.

His daughter, Helen, said that his years as president, "were the only unhappy years of his entire life." Despite years of public service, he was ill prepared for the presidency; he was frequently indecisive, and the public thought him lazy. Roosevelt had decided not to seek another term in 1908, all but giving the office to Taft. But Roosevelt missed the presidency, and, as Taft's term wore on, Roosevelt began to find fault with his policies.

As Roosevelt's criticism grew, Taft was surprised, then hurt, then bitter. He did not understand why Roosevelt had turned against him. Roosevelt probably had no good reason for criticizing Taft, other than Taft had the job Roosevelt wanted.

In 1912, Roosevelt entered the race for the Republican nomination against Taft. Roosevelt had widespread support from the voters, but Taft had the backing of the party professionals, who would decide the nominee. Taft won the nomination, but still Roosevelt would not quit, organizing a third party and dividing the Republican vote just enough to give Democratic candidate Woodrow Wilson the election.

The disappointment of losing an office he had never really wanted disappeared quickly, and as 1913 began he wrote, "The nearer I get to the inauguration of my successor, the greater the relief I feel." There were some reservations about his life out of power, "Doubtless later on I shall have a restlessness . . . growing out of the absence of the excitement of a strenuous political life."

A lifetime of public service had given Taft power but not a great deal of money. As his term ended, he gave more and more thought to what he would do to earn a living. His wife had managed to save $100,000 during his White House years, but he would need more.

At first, he thought of returning to his law practice, telling a friend, "I don't see that there is anything left for me to do." The problem was that Taft had not practiced law for nearly three decades, and even then he was a mediocre attorney. Fortunately, Yale University offered him a law professorship which paid $5,000 a year. Combined with his savings and money from lectures it would allow him to live comfortably.

Before leaving the White House, Taft spoke to a New York club, looking humorously upon the plight of expresidents. "What are we to do with our ex-presidents?" he asked.

> The proper and scientific administration of a dose of chloroform or of the fruit of the lotos tree, and the reduction of the flesh of the thus quietly departed to ashes in a funeral pyre to satisfy the wishes of friends and families, might make a fitting end to the life of one who has held the highest office, and at the same time would secure the country from the troublesome fear that the occupant could ever come back.

Andrew Carnegie, aware of the financial problems of former presidents, offered a pension of $25,000 to Taft and others who had served as president. Taft saw problems in accepting a pension from one of the nation's leading industrialists. He wrote to his brother, Charles, "I can't take the pension for obvious reasons, but I think the old man wanted to do the right thing."

Almost from the moment he lost the election, there was talk of his running again in 1916, but Taft put an end to it. "I do not share with you the view that there is any probability of my being selected as a candidate for the Republicans at the end of four years. I have proven to be a burdensome leader and not one that aroused the multitude, not one that was calculated to lead on to victory in a close contest."

After Wilson's inauguration, Taft left for a month of vacation in the South, playing golf at Augusta. Then, he moved to New Haven, Connecticut to take up his duties at Yale.

It was a perfect job for Taft, giving him a base of operation but hardly taxing him. He delivered two lectures a week at 5 P.M. on Monday and Friday. His first class attracted 100 students, primarily because they wanted to hear a former president. But the class sizes declined year after year because his lectures were predictable and often boring. Still, it drew some students because Taft was an easy grader, and there was little discipline in the class.

Taft was seldom in New Haven, finding that he could make impressive money on the lecture circuit. His fees ranged from $150 to $1,000 for a speech. There were also magazine articles for the *Ladies Home Journal* and *Saturday Evening Post* usually for $1,000 and regular columns for the Philadelphia *Public Ledger*. Taft, who a few months earlier was worried about money, found himself making more money than he ever had. He adjusted easily to retirement, telling a friend, "You don't know how much fun it is to sit back . . . and watch the playing of the game down there in Washington, without any responsibility of my own."

To another friend he said, "I wish to keep as far in the background as I can. I have grown fully used to reading the papers without my name in them, and it is not an unpleasant change."

Like other former presidents, Taft quickly became a critic of his successor. He said Wilson was "as much an opportunist as anybody we have had in the White House."

In 1914, Taft briefly considered returning to politics, this time as a candidate for the House of Representatives from New Haven. Taft seriously considered the idea because he thought he might secure a seat on the judiciary committee and push some of his ideas for judicial reform. "If I could get on the Judiciary Committee in the House, I believe I might make a fuss on the subject." In the end, he decided against making the race; he was happy in New Haven and no longer had political aspirations. "I think I have been in the public eye long enough."

Although he had no desire to return to politics, he still harbored one desire, the same desire he had held for years, to sit on the Supreme Court. From time to time, he thought Wilson might name him to the court. Taft had named a Democrat to the court, and he hoped that Wilson would be willing to name a Republican. Wilson would not.

When World War I came, Taft joined in supporting Wilson and was named to the chairmanship of the National War Labor Board, which was designed to negotiate employer-employee disputes to insure that there was no interruption in the flow of vital war materials. Labor and management each had five members on the board, and Taft was the eleventh and deciding member.

Taft's experience on the board brought him into contact with working men and women for the first time, and it had a strong impact. After a tour of the South, he told the executive secretary of the board, "Why didn't you tell me about the conditions down there?" The executive secretary, W. Jett Lauck, told Taft he had tried to tell him, but Taft would not listen. "You didn't tell me anything. Why, I had no idea. How can people live on such wages?" In decision after decision, Taft ordered wages increased, becoming one of the board's most prolabor members.

Taft continued to gaze longingly at the Supreme Court, but Wilson would not appoint him. When the Senate delayed passage of Wilson's League of Nations proposal, Taft campaigned for it in 15 states. His Republican friends could not understand his helping Wilson. "I don't like Wilson any better than you do, but I think I can rise above my personal attitude . . . in order to help along the world and the country." When the league went down to defeat, he blamed Wilson, "that mulish enigma, that mountain of egotism and selfishness who lives in the White House."

In 1920, Republican Warren G. Harding was elected president, and Taft's hopes for a Supreme Court seat soared. After Harding's election, Taft was invited to visit Harding's Ohio home and give advice on forming an administration. After they had talked for a while, Harding stunned Taft by asking, "By the way, I want to ask you, would you accept a position on the Supreme Bench because if you would, I'll put you on that court."

Taft wrote his wife, "I said it was and always had been the ambition of my life." Taft said that because he had been president, he did not think he could accept an appointment as an associate justice, only as chief justice. Harding said nothing more about the appointment.

Unfortunately for Taft, there was already a chief justice, a man Taft had named to the court. But two months after Harding became president, Chief Justice Edward D. White died. Harding kept his promise and nominated Taft for chief justice. The appointment overjoyed Taft, who wrote, "The truth is that in my present life I don't remember that I ever was president."

When he had been president, critics had said he was lazy; as chief justice, he would show everyone that he was not lazy. He began rising at 5:15 every morning, working on cases at his home until breakfast at eight. To keep his weight down, he walked to the court, and when he returned home he worked on cases until ten. The pace was hectic and could not be continued. His health began to decline, and after five years, Taft reduced his workload. Still, he did more than his share of the work, writing more opinions than any other justice.

The court he presided over was respectable if not outstanding. It was marked by serious divisions, split between the conservatives Taft himself had appointed and the more liberal members named by Wilson.

He dropped the morning walks as a concession to his poor health and became all too aware of his advancing age. "One of my constant duties is to look over the necrology of the morning papers, and I feel sorry to find in almost every issue the account of the death of some friend of mine."

He had been overweight most of his life, and his heart had grown weary of pumping blood through his large body. In 1928, there were growing signs that the end was coming. In January 1930, he began hallucinating, unable to tell where he was. He was brought back to Washington from a vacation in North Carolina. At Union Station he was lifted off the train, unable to walk. Slowly his life faded and on February 2 he submitted his resignation to President Herbert Hoover. He lay in his bed, unable to do anything for himself, unaware of those around him. On March 8, 1930, at the age of 72, he died.

Woodrow Wilson

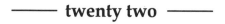

—— twenty two ——

How quickly fortunes changed for Woodrow Wilson. When World War I ended, Wilson went to France to negotiate a peace that he thought would last. The cornerstone of that peace would be the League of Nations, a world body dedicated to insuring that there would never again be a world war. In Europe, he was hailed as a great leader: crowds turned out to cheer him as the man who had helped win one war and would prevent future wars.

Back in the United States, Wilson assumed that the Senate would approve his treaty, but Republican opposition to the league formed and, in an effort to save his dream, Wilson launched a nationwide campaign to rally support. The hectic pace was too much for him, and in Pueblo, Colorado, he broke down. He was taken back to Washington where he suffered a stroke one week later, leaving his left side paralyzed. He had 17 months remaining in his second term, but his health was so fragile his wife Edith assumed most of his duties. Edith Bolling Galt Wilson had married Wilson in 1915 after the death of Wilson's first wife.

There was doubt that Wilson would live to see the end of his term, but increasingly his thoughts turned to seeking a third term. The idea shocked his friends, who tried to hint that he should drop the plan. Wilson told his physician that should the convention become deadlocked, "In such circumstances I would feel obliged to accept the nomination." The convention opened in San Francisco with Wilson's son-in-law, William McAdoo, showing the greatest strength. Most of Wilson's aides, realizing the nature of his health, were working secretly against Wilson's nomination. There was one exception, Secretary of State Bainbridge Colby, who worked for Wilson behind the scenes. Postmaster General A.S. Burleson, realizing that Wilson's nomination would be a disaster for Wilson and the party, telegraphed the White House urging Wilson to endorse his son-in-law. Wilson went into a rage and threatened to fire Burleson.

Colby planned to wait until the convention became hopelessly deadlocked to bring Wilson's name to the floor. The other Cabinet members learned of Colby's plan and descended upon him, calling him cruel for pushing a sick man into a campaign that would surely kill him. At last, Colby yielded; he would drop his efforts, but would not let Wilson know what he was doing. He telegraphed Wilson that the time was not right for his name to be submitted. After 43 ballots, the convention turned to Governor James Cox of Ohio. The news sent Wilson into another rage as he screamed obscenities, this from a man who had seldom sworn.

The bitterness continued throughout the campaign; Wilson did little to help Cox, even though Cox supported Wilson's policies. On election day, the president planned to stay up two hours past his nine o'clock bedtime to hear the results. There was no need. By nine it was all over: Cox had suffered a humiliating defeat. The nation not only rejected Cox, it rejected Wilson and his plan for a League of Nations, and Wilson sank deeper into despondency, issuing no statement, unable to understand what had happened.

A casual friend sent a message saying he and many others still supported the president and would continue to follow his lead. Wilson replied, "I thank him, but there is nowhere to go."

Wilson and his wife had four months remaining in the White House, and almost immediately they began to search for a new home. They considered moving to New York, Richmond, Baltimore, Boston, or staying in Washington. They finally decided to remain in Washington, Mrs. Wilson's hometown and the home of many of their friends.

In December 1920, he was awarded the Nobel Peace Prize, but his poor health ruled out a trip to Sweden to accept it.

Mrs. Wilson went house hunting, finally settling on a large house at 2340 S Street. The purchase price was nearly $150,000, but $100,000 of the money came from ten friends who put up $10,000 apiece. She arranged for the installation of an electric elevator to carry her husband from floor to floor.

As his term drew to a close, Wilson met individually with the members of his cabinet to thank them for their service. When he met with Secretary of State Colby, he asked, "Well, Colby, what are you doing to do?"

Colby said, "I suppose I shall return to New York and open a musty law office again, which, after this experience, will be a dreary business. But I must make a living."

To Colby's surprise, Wilson said, "Well, I too must make a living. As I was once a lawyer, why not open an office together here." Colby was stunned, leaping to his feet and saying, "Do you really mean that, Mr. President?"

Wilson said that he did indeed mean it. "I can't face a life of idleness, besides, I must do something to add to my income." He was worth between $300,000 and $600,000. As president, he was given $25,000 a year for entertaining expenses, but because of the war he did no entertaining and pocketed the money.

Inauguration Day came, and Wilson and his wife moved to the house on S Street. To ease the transition, his wife had a duplicate of the Lincoln bed made for Wilson and purchased the Pierce-Arrow he had used as president.

His days became predictable, breakfast in his bedroom, then down the electric elevator to the first floor where he went through the mail with his secretary, back to his room for lunch, perhaps a guest in the afternoon, followed by a ride in the Pierce-Arrow, dinner in the library, and by nine he was in his room for a massage, then bed.

There were scores of business suggestions, all of which Wilson rejected. Most asked him to write books: one offered $150,000 for a history of the peace negotiations. The Ladies Home Journal offered $5,000 each for a series of articles and a syndicate offered him a newspaper column. To an offer to write an autobiography, Wilson replied, "There ain't going to be none." At first, they retained a guard to keep the curious away, but there were no curious: no one wanted to see the former president, and after a month the guard was dismissed.

Several months after Wilson's term ended, the offices of Wilson & Colby opened for business; they were elaborate suites in both New York and Washington, and from the first, prospective clients were standing in line to enlist the services of the new firm. The government of Ecuador asked for help in obtaining a $12,000,000 loan, the Western Ukrainian Republic wanted assistance in being recognized by the League of Nations, even members of the Warren G. Harding administration attempted to hire the firm to represent them in the Teapot Dome scandal. In all, hundreds of thousands of dollars in fees were offered, but to all Wilson said no. He would accept no case which would bring dishonor to his former position or force him to use his influence.

After the first year, the firm had lost thousands of dollars. Wilson himself made $5,000, but Colby lost a great deal. He had underwritten the cost of the offices and other expenses, but Wilson had visited the offices only once. From the start it had been a bad idea. Wilson had no strong interest in practicing law; he had practiced briefly decades before in Atlanta but did not like the work and was not particularly good at it. He returned to college to earn his doctorate. Finally, Colby gave up, asking Wilson if the firm could be dissolved, and Wilson agreed.

There was one short-lived attempt to write a book on government, but Wilson never got beyond the dedication to his wife:

A Dedication
to
E.B.W.

I dedicate this book because it is a book in which I have tried to interpret life, the life of a nation, and she has shown me the full meaning of life. Her heart is not only true but wise; her thoughts are not only free but touched with vision; she teaches and guides by being what she is; her unconscious interpretation of faith and duty makes all the way clear; her power to comprehend makes work and thought alike easier, and more near to what it seeks.

His health improved only slightly, but it was enough to permit him to begin going to the theatre once a week to see the vaudeville show. He went every Saturday night, always sitting in the same seat, and the patrons at Keith's Theatre began to call it "Wilson Night."

In 1923, his eyesight began to fail, and his wife had to begin reading to him. Slowly, the mood of the people began to change as the corruption of the Harding administration became public. On the evening before Armistice Day in 1923, Wilson made a nationwide radio address from his home. It was a tortured performance: unable to memorize the speech and unable to read it, he was prompted by his wife, whose voice could be heard in the background. But his words were strong, although his voice was weak.

> Memories of that happy time are forever marred and embittered for us by the shameful fact that when the victory was won . . . we withdrew into a sullen and selfish isolation which is manifestly ignoble because it is manifestly dishonorable. The only way in which we can worthily give proof of our appreciation of the high significance of Armistice Day is by resolving to put self-interest away and once more formulate and act upon the highest ideals and purposes of international policy. Thus, and only thus, can we return to the true traditions of America.

His speech was over, but radio was new to him, and he was not sure what to say. He looked at his wife and said, "That is all, isn't it?" His words carried throughout the nation. The next morning crowds began to gather outside Wilson's home, growing each hour until more tha 20,000 people jammed the street. A little band showed up to play, and finally Wilson came out, his weight supported by his cane. He was clearly overcome by the crowd. He spoke briefly about World War I, then said, "Thank you with all my heart for your kindness." He turned away and said, "That's all I can do." He turned to go inside his house then turned back to speak again. His voice became stronger, his tone more urgent as he said:

> Just one word more; I cannot refrain from saying it. I am not one of those that have the least anxiety about the triumph of principles I have stood for. I have seen fools resist Providence before, and I have seen their destruction, as will come upon these again, utter destruction and contempt. That we shall prevail is as sure as that God reigns. Thank you.

In the campaign of 1920, Harding had offered a return to normalcy, but as his administration became discredited, it was Wilson whose popularity grew. He had lived to see his reputation restored, although he would never see the United States join the League of Nations. That would have to wait more than two decades: for the nation to fight in another World War and spur the creation of the United Nations.

In 1923, Harding died, a certain surprise that the seriously ill Wilson had outlived the man who seemed to be in robust health. But life was slowly slipping away from Wilson. In 1924 his condition grew worse. He was confined to his bed, barely able to understand what was happening around him. At times he was lucid, even joking with his doctors, but most of the time he was barely able to speak. "I am a broken piece of machinery. When the machinery is broken. . . ," but he did not have enough strength to finish the sentence.

Word leaked out that Wilson was dying, and people began to come to his house, standing quietly outside. On Saturday, February 2, Wilson's doctor came outside to talk with the reporters. "Mr. Wilson realizes his fight is over. He is making a game effort. It almost breaks one down. He is very brave. He is just slowly ebbing away."

The next day, his sight and hearing gone, he said his last word, calling for his wife, "Edith."

At 11:15 A.M. on February 3, 1924, Wilson died at the age of 67.

Calvin Coolidge

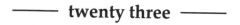

twenty three

In 1927, President Calvin Coolidge announced that he would not seek reelection. The announcement came as a surprise, and left a number of people unconvinced. For several months, in private conversations, Coolidge assured his supporters that he meant what he said and would not change his mind. He told one friend, "I've been here about long enough." To another he said, "There are plenty of other good men around." There were still doubters, and on December 6, Coolidge told the Republican National Committee, "My statement stands. No one should be led to suppose that I have modified it. My decision will be respected."

His philosophy of thrifty government was popular enough to ensure the election of another Republican, Herbert Hoover. In his final message to Congress, Coolidge again warned of the error of government extravagance. His popularity as he left office was as high as when he had taken over on the death of Warren G. Harding in 1923.

Following the inauguration of Hoover, Coolidge and his wife drove to Union Station and made a brief statement, "Good-bye, I have had a very enjoyable time in Washington." He turned to leave and then noticing the dozens of reporters who surrounded him said, "I'm not getting much private life."

There had been a great deal of speculation about what Coolidge would do after leaving the White House. He had said nothing about his plans. There were rumors that he would become a college president, take over the presidency at a life insurance company, run for the Senate, or even take a seat on the Supreme Court, although he was not an attorney, and there was no opening.

Coolidge and his wife returned to their home in Northampton, Massachusetts, where a crowd of 3,000 turned out to cheer their neighbor. After the welcoming ceremonies, Coolidge went to his home, a seven-room, two-family house, which he had rented throughout his presidency for $32 a month.

Quickly, the modest home became a tourist attraction, with cars streaming down the small street in hopes of catching a glance of the former president. Whenever he ventured out to sit on the front porch, a crowd quickly gathered, and Coolidge was forced to retreat back into the house. Finally, he gave up; the crowds forced him to move to a twelve-room house located on a nine-acre site which would give him the privacy he wanted.

Before leaving the White House, Coolidge began writing his memoirs in response to a request from *Cosmopolitan* magazine. The magazine serialized the autobiography for several months, then published it as a book. It proved to be a big moneymaker for Coolidge. Not only did he receive royalties from the book, but he worked a deal with bookstores to pay him one dollar to autograph a copy of the book. Coolidge turned over the profits from the autographs to his wife's church. In all, he made some $75,000 from the autobiography.

He also wrote three articles for *Ladies Home Journal* on the subject of peace, and his wife wrote a number of articles on the duties of the first lady.

Coolidge moved easily into a leisurely routine. He slept each morning until eight; then his chauffeur drove him to his office in the Masonic Building where his secretary had the mail sorted and ready for Coolidge. At noon, he went home for lunch and an afternoon nap, returned to his office about two-thirty, and remained until four.

One of his hobbies was counting tourists. He kept track of the visitors who passed by his house. When a reporter asked him if there were many tourists, he said, "Not as many as yesterday, there were 163 then."

In the winter of 1929–30, Coolidge and his wife took a trip to Florida as part of a conference sponsored by the New York Life Insurance Company. Then they went to California by way of New Orleans.

But as Coolidge traveled, the nation was changing. The stock market crash in October 1929 had thrown the nation into a depression. The economic principles that Coolidge had lived by were being discredited.

In June of 1930, Coolidge began writing a syndicated column for the McClure Newspaper Syndicate. The columns each ran about 200 words and were titled, "Thinking Things over with Calvin Coolidge." He received $2,400 a week for the columns, which were little more than aimless platitudes on the virtues of faith, work, and a sound economic system. For Coolidge, the columns became a chore he dreaded; he was reluctant to speak out forcefully and as soon as his one-year contract expired he called an end to the project.

Coolidge joined the board of the New York Life Insurance Company shortly after leaving the White House. He looked forward to attending the monthly meetings, which paid him $50 plus expenses. He believed in the importance of life insurance, and that was what led Coolidge to agree to give a radio commercial for the company.

The commercial was mild; Coolidge spoke out against insurance agents who urged customers to change repeatedly their policies. New York Life had the speech printed into pamphlets, and Coolidge became the first former president to become a spokesman for a corporation.

But his career was short lived. A St. Louis insurance agent named Lewis G. Tebbetts sued Coolidge for $100,000. Tebbetts claimed that Coolidge had damaged his reputation by speaking out against agents who turned over policies to gain greater commissions. Tebbetts had little chance of winning the suit, but Coolidge did not want to get involved in a court fight which would bring publicity. After some negotiations, Coolidge and Tebbetts agreed to settle out of court with Coolidge paying $2,500 for Tebbett's legal expenses.

The Depression grew worse and the election of 1932 approached. More and more, Coolidge sat alone in his office, staring out the window and rocking. He became bitter as the attacks on his economic policies increased, and those whom he had considered friends did nothing to defend him.

As Hoover's popularity fell, some Republicans began to search for an alternative to lead the party, and Coolidge was frequently mentioned. He wanted no part of the effort and told his friend William F. Whiting, "When you get to Chicago [site of the Republican convention] I am depending on you to see that nothing of this kind happens to me. It won't do."

Whiting replied by sending Coolidge an editorial from a newspaper that urged Coolidge to run. Coolidge replied, "I have done all that I can do. Others must now carry on the government. Just drop me."

Hoover was renominated but was in serious trouble in his battle with Franklin D. Roosevelt. Hoover asked Coolidge to help, but Coolidge was reluctant. He did write an article for the *Saturday Evening Post* extolling Hoover, "We know that he is safe and sound."

But Coolidge was unwilling to do more, despite pleas from the Republican National Committee. He wrote to a friend, "Everybody that has a cause wants me to make a speech. I have said all I know in the article which I have already prepared."

Finally Coolidge gave into the pressure and agreed to speak at Madison Square Garden on October 11, 1932. A crowd of 19,000 turned out for the speech which was also broadcast nationwide on radio. The speech did not go well; when Coolidge began by saying, "When I was in Washington . . .," the audience laughed. He did not understand them, and they no longer understood him.

He went back home, determined to do nothing more for the Hoover campaign. He wrote:

> I feel I no longer fit in with these times. Great changes can come in four years. These socialistic notions of government are not of my day. . . . It has always seemed to me that common sense is the real solvent for the nation's problems at all times, common sense and hard work. When I read of the newfangled things that are now so popular I realize that my time in public affairs is past. I wouldn't know how to handle them if I were called upon to do so.

The election results left him depressed; his policies had been rejected in the Roosevelt landslide. On New Year's Day 1933, Coolidge had dinner with friends and showed how despondent he had become. He said that the world was in a perilous state and that nothing was permanent except religion. On Thursday, January 5, he went to his office as usual, but at ten o'clock he told his secretary he wanted to go home for lunch earlier than usual. As he entered the house, his wife was on her way out to do some shopping. Around noon, he went upstairs to his bedroom to shave. His wife returned a few minutes later and went upstairs to find him lying on his back. Death had come instantly from a coronary thrombosis at the age of sixty-one.

Herbert Hoover

—— twenty four ——

Even Franklin Roosevelt once said that Herbert Hoover would make a good president. It seemed as though no man was better to assume the presidency than Hoover. Following World War I, he had directed efforts to feed millions of Europeans, then served as secretary of commerce under Harding and Coolidge before being elected president. He took office in 1929 in the midst of a national boom that made stock market players out of nearly everyone. Then, in October 1929, the stock market crashed, setting in motion a chain reaction that plunged the nation into its worst depression.

Hoover, who just one year before had seemed so prepared, now seemed totally unprepared, unsure what to do to solve the worsening depression. Not only were his policies ineffective, but Hoover's personality did little to inspire confidence: his manner was cold and aloof. Friendly journalists felt a need to point out that Hoover had a sense of humor and could be quite human.

Through 1930 and 1931, conditions continued to grow worse, and Hoover's popularity plummeted. In 1932, the Republicans stuck with Hoover, and the Democrats nominated Roosevelt, the New York governor. An incumbent president had not been turned out of office in nearly half a century, and at first, Hoover believed he would win reelection despite the Depression.

In September, Maine voters handed the Democrats a victory for the first time since before the Civil War, electing a Democratic governor and two senators. The Republicans knew they were in trouble, and Hoover dropped his strategy of campaigning from the

White House and got out among the voters. Reporters were invited to his retreat in Virginia to take pictures of a grim-faced Hoover sitting astride a horse, obviously unhappy, but hoping it would make him more popular with the voters.

Then came the long nationwide tour, and he told friends, ". . . this fight isn't over yet. We have just started. I shall fight every inch of the way." But it was a doomed campaign, and everyone except Hoover knew it. On election night, Hoover was at his home in Palo Alto, California where the students gathered around his house to cheer the former Stanford student. At 9:17 P.M., Hoover conceded defeat. The next morning, he faced reporters and said, "No doubt you are ravenous for news, and I haven't got it. I just got up from the best night's sleep I have had in a week."

For most presidents who are turned out of office, the greatest pain comes on election day, then passes as they spend the last months of their term quietly waiting to turn over the government to a new man. But for Hoover, there was no quiet, no respite from the Depression. In February, the banks began to close, and Hoover briefly considered assuming some type of wartime powers to bring the situation under control. Hoover tried desperately; at times he almost begged Roosevelt to join him in making some type of statement. Hoover knew that he was powerless, but he hoped that with Roosevelt's help he might be able to stop the slide.

Two days before the inauguration, Hoover met with Roosevelt at the White House and again asked for his support, but Roosevelt would not give it and the meeting degenerated. Finally, Roosevelt said, "Mr. President, I know it is customary to do so, but you don't have to return our call if you don't want to."

Hoover was insulted and in anger said, "Mr. Roosevelt, when you have been in Washington as long as I have, you will learn that the President of the United States calls on nobody." With that he turned quickly and headed out the door.

On Inauguration Day, Hoover told an aide sadly, "We are at the end of our string. There is nothing more we can do."

Hoover and Roosevelt rode together to the Capitol, Roosevelt trying to make conversation, but giving up when Hoover said nothing. Roosevelt took the oath of office and Hoover departed immediately for Union Station and the train ride to New York. Hoover said he would remain in New York for a few days in case Roosevelt had any questions, but a call from Roosevelt never came;

there was nothing the new president wanted from Herbert Hoover.

Hoover had trouble understanding why there was no call; incoming presidents always had questions, even if they were only about the quality of the White House servants. Woodrow Wilson, after defeating William Howard Taft, had asked the outgoing president for advice.

Nearly 20 years later, in an article for *Collier's,* Hoover would reflect back on his departure.

> Democracy is not a polite employer. . . . When a President is out he carries no pension, privilege or pomp. He does not even carry away an honorary title, not even colonel. He is about the only retired official who is just Mister. . . . Mrs. Hoover and I found abundant compensations from being kicked out of a job after nearly 40 years of administrative responsibility and 20 years of strenuous public service. . . . It was emancipation from a sort of peonage—a revolution back to personal freedom. . . . There were no scores of visitors to see at 15-minute intervals, most of whom wanted something for themselves that they ought not have.

In late March, Hoover went back to California to his home in Palo Alto. The years of public service had drained his once healthy fortune, and he had to decide how he would earn money. In his memoirs, he wrote:

> The problem of post-White House living has proved difficult for many former Presidents to solve. There are but small pickings for lawyers and engineers except from corporate connections. The alternatives are to become a columnist and crowd some worthy workman out of press. Or take soap or insurance or pull money for broadcasting news comments. Or become a merchant or an industrial executive. Or undertake payment for public speaking. Any of these alternatives means more or less exploitation of the office of President.

He joined the board of the New York Life Insurance Company, a job which required little but paid well. He also depended upon the generosity of his friends for support.

During World War I, Hoover had read a book about the thousands of documents that had been lost during the confusion following the French Revolution. He did not want the same thing to happen to the papers of World War I, and he set up a library at Stanford to collect the documents. During his years in the cabinet and as president, he had been unable to devote time to the project and now had plenty of spare time.

Life for Herbert Hoover was different than for other former presidents. His name was no longer synonymous with service to his nation but with depression and despair. The Republicans wanted to forget him, and the Democrats wanted his memory kept alive only to use as a whipping boy when elections rolled around.

He had 30 newspapers airmailed to his home each day, keeping up with the latest developments, but no one asked for his opinions. He wanted desperately to speak out against Roosevelt's policies, but realized that few would listen. Finally, in 1934, he moved back to New York, to live most of the year at the Waldorf Astoria, thinking that this would put him back in the mainstream of events.

That same year, he wrote his first attack on the New Deal, called "The Challenge to Liberty." He told friends that the New Deal was creating a "fascist-Nazi state," and said the Civilian Conservation Corps was "laying plans for a new military arm of the government." He compared the AAA to the agricultural programs of Hitler and criticized the tyranny of the NRA.

Hoover suffered another setback in the elections of 1934 as Democratic candidates campaigned against him, calling his name to frighten voters into the Democratic ranks. Hoover's views of the Roosevelt policies were spoken in personal bitterness, not because he really opposed them. Thomas Dewey once told Hoover, "I have a suspicion that you would have signed practically all the legislation that F.D.R. signed." Hoover thought a moment and said, "I think I would have."

Hoover actually took some of the credit for the New Deal laws, telling journalist Mark Sullivan, ". . . I think it might be entertaining to the public to trace out the origins of a large number of these new Deal things. . . ." His conclusion was that they originated with the Republicans and Congress had not passed them because of Democratic opposition.

Although he was a strong critic of Roosevelt, he was not ready to sign on with the Liberty Lobby, a group of the most reactionary Republicans. He was a leader in the fight against Roosevelt's plan to enlarge the membership of the Supreme Court by adding justices more favorable to the New Deal. He organized groups in 20 states to battle the Roosevelt plan, and in February 1937 he went on nationwide radio to voice his opposition.

Hoover was seeking vindication, hoping that somehow the public would see that his course had been the right one: that if he had only been allowed another term everything would have turned out all right. In 1935, he went on a speaking tour which he hoped would revive his popularity and indicate his availability for a draft in 1936. But there was no interest in Hoover at the 1936 convention. The delegates gave him a warm reception when he spoke, comparing the New Deal with European dictatorships, but the delegates gave the nomination to Alf Landon, a man Hoover had little use for.

Hoover was so disdained that Landon refused to send him a written request to give speeches during the campaign. Landon did call Hoover with the request, but when reporters found out about the call, Landon denied having made it. Landon went down to the same humiliating defeat Hoover had suffered four years earlier. Hoover saw a new opening for his party's leadership: perhaps 1940 would be his year to return to power. In 1937, he spent $100,000 of his own money to finance Republican activities and spoke in 16 states. Nearly every day he held a news conference somewhere to push his views that Roosevelt was seizing too much power.

In 1938, Hoover went to Europe and visited Adolph Hitler. He was careful not to be photographed too close to Hitler and told a friend that Hitler was "partly insane." In Poland he condemned Hitler and upon returning to New York became one of the first to speak out against Nazi treatment of the Jews. Still, he maintained strong isolationist views and was opposed to the United States becoming involved in the worsening European situation. But, as he had in World War I, he was primarily concerned with the civilian victims of the war and raised $6 million for Polish and Finnish relief.

Once the United States entered the war, Hoover gave it his full support then settled down to write a book, "The Problems of Lasting Peace," in 1942 and in 1945 "The Basis of Lasting Peace." The first volume contained 50 suggestions for keeping the peace.

In 1945, Roosevelt died, and, in a strange way, the death had a dramatic impact on Hoover. For a dozen years, Roosevelt had been the center of Hoover's life; nothing the president did was right in Hoover's opinion: everything he did was somehow a slap at the former president. Hoover's feelings against Roosevelt were so strong that he refused to set foot in Washington while Roosevelt was in the White House.

Two months after Roosevelt's death, Hoover sent a memorandum to President Harry Truman on ending the war. It was the first step in his return to public service. He visited Truman in the White House and at the president's request took responsibility for food relief in areas affected by the war. He was back at his old post again, just as he had been after World War I. He traveled 35,000 miles, fighting famine in war-ravished countries. In 1947, Congress reversed a slap at Hoover that had hurt him deeply. Roosevelt's interior secretary, Harold L. Ickes, changed the name of Hoover Dam to Boulder Dam, but with Truman in the White House, Congress voted unanimously to restore the original name. Hoover had always been an unusual Republican; like Dwight Eisenhower in 1952, no one had been quite sure whether he was a Republican or Democrat until he ran for president. Now, as he emerged again, he was a mix of conservative Republican and liberal Democrat.

He opposed military intervention in Korea and favored withdrawing U.S. forces from Europe. He did favor the expulsion of the Soviet Union from the United Nations, but refused an invitation from Truman to chair a committee to investigate communists in government saying, "I doubt if there are any consequential card-carrying communists in the Government."

He did accept another offer from Truman, in 1947, to chair a commission to streamline the executive branch of government. It was a post Hoover had sought since 1921 when he first urged President Warren Harding to create such a plan. He had tried unsuccessfully to organize such a commission when he was president. Hoover went to work with the aid of several hundred experts and his report resulted in substantial savings. More importantly, it changed the relationship between Congress and the president by strengthening the resources of the executive branch.

There was another commission under Eisenhower, but Eisenhower was startled by suggestions such as selling the Tennessee Valley Authority. He sat on most of the recommendations until they were outdated. The lack of action turned Hoover against Eisenhower, the first Republican to serve since Hoover was defeated two decades earlier. Hoover predicted that Eisenhower would rank with Coolidge as president, unable to admit to himself that a far more cutting insult would be to compare Eisenhower with himself.

Hoover was an early backer of Richard Nixon, but somehow the relationship soured. Asked later how he felt about Nixon, Hoover replied, "How do you think I feel? I'm among those who persuaded him to run for Congress in the first place." Hoover was a longtime friend of Joseph P. Kennedy and may have actually favored the election of John Kennedy in the 1960 election.

Hoover was in his eighties, going blind and deaf. When asked what expresidents did, he said, "We spend our time taking pills and dedicating libraries." He had outlived most of his contemporaries, and after the death of his wife in 1944 he was alone much of the time.

In 1964, Hoover endorsed the Republican nominee, Barry Goldwater, although the endorsement was lukewarm and it was clear Hoover was doing nothing more than being a loyal Republican. Just three weeks later, Hoover died of cancer at the age of ninety-one. He had lived 31 years after leaving the presidency, longer than any other president, and except for John Quincy Adams was the longest-living president. He was buried with his wife in West Branch, Iowa.

Harry Truman

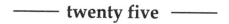

Harry Truman, at times one of the most popular presidents in history and at other times one of the most unpopular, decided not to run for reelection in 1952, but he never stopped being a politician. He was controversial to the end, seeking to dominate the Democratic Party and the candidates who ran under its banner. He briefly considered running again in 1952 but was discouraged by his aides who realized that his administration was in serious trouble.

Truman threw his support to Illinois Governor Adlai Stevenson but almost immediately began to feud with Stevenson. Because of his upset victory in 1948, Truman felt he knew the secret to winning presidential elections and became increasingly angry as Stevenson ignored his advice. Truman wrote, but never mailed, a series of letters to Stevenson, expressing his anger. In one, he said, "I have come to the conclusion that you are embarrassed by having the President of the United States in your corner. . . . Therefore I shall remain silent and stay in Washington until Nov. 4."

Eisenhower won easily, touching off a feud between Truman and Eisenhower. On Inauguration Day in 1953, Truman planned a luncheon for the new president at the White House, but Eisenhower refused the invitation, a slight Truman remembered for years. When Eisenhower arrived at the White House to pick up Truman for the trip to the Capitol, Truman waited for Eisenhower to leave his car, but Eisenhower stayed put, forcing Truman to come to him.

The conversation during the drive to the Capitol was bitter. Truman later wrote that Eisenhower sat in silence for a few minutes, then said, "I did not attend your inauguration in 1949 out of consideration for you because if I had been present I would have drawn attention away from you."

Truman, already in a nasty mood, snapped back, "You were not here in 1949 because I did not send for you. But if I had sent for you, you would have come."

Truman clearly enjoyed being president. Outspoken and accessible to the press, he was always there for a snappy one-liner or biting comment. After the inauguration, Truman attended a small luncheon in his honor and said to a former aide, "Two hours ago, I could have said five words and been quoted in fifteen minutes in every capital of the world. Now I could talk for two hours and nobody would give a damn."

He had no interest in becoming an elder statesman; he was, he said time and again, a politician and his cause was the Democratic Party. Almost immediately, he began giving advice to Eisenhower, using the newspapers to relay his messages, since Eisenhower had no intention of seeing Truman personally. He said that Eisenhower was not being tough enough in dealing with Congress and needed to assert himself more.

Truman was sixty-eight years old, but hardly ready to retire to the quiet life in Independence, Missouri. Despite the nomination of Adlai Stevenson, Truman remained the titular head of the party; his speeches were carried on nationwide radio and printed in leading newspapers. Everywhere Truman went, he gave informal news conferences, which quickly found their way onto the front pages. For Truman, the Republicans could do nothing right. He accused the administration of blundering in foreign affairs and said Eisenhower had "shown his incapacity to govern."

As the 1956 campaign approached, he stepped up his attacks on Eisenhower, speaking out everywhere on the theme that the Democrats could win the White House back. There were some who suggested that Truman might be the candidate to run against Eisenhower, but Truman brushed aside those suggestions and, in 1955, said Adlai Stevenson would be the best candidate.

Truman did not limit his criticism to Eisenhower; he charged that Vice-President Richard Nixon had once called him a traitor, although there was no evidence to support Truman's charge. Truman said he would refuse to meet Nixon again. "It would just start a fight." In 1956, Truman went on a tour of Europe, but once again his mind was on politics. At a news conference in Salzburg, Austria, he said, "I believe anybody we nominate can beat Eisenhower, and I think he should be beaten."

Truman, who had drawn Republican criticism for not being tough enough in dealing with the communists, turned the tables, saying it was Eisenhower who was failing to inform the American people about the communist threat. He thought Eisenhower's style was too reserved and thought his policies were damaging the nation.

As the years went by, Truman's influence began to wane. It seemed that, to compensate, he spoke more loudly to gain the attention he had once commanded with a single phrase. In 1956, speaking in Des Moines, he said the Eisenhower administration had "one of the most amazing records of political betrayal I have ever seen." Harking back to the 1948 campaign when he had scored political gains by branding the 80th Congress "the do-nothing Congress," Truman called Eisenhower a do-nothing president.

Truman had already endorsed Stevenson for the 1956 Democratic nomination, but as the convention neared, he began having second thoughts. Privately, he liked New York Governor Averell Harriman and on the eve of the convention switched his endorsement from Stevenson to Harriman. He called Stevenson a conservative who lacked fighting spirit. But Truman had misjudged his influence and the strength of Stevenson, who won easily on the first ballot. Truman had overplayed his hand and lost his place as the nation's leading Democrat. The crowds that had surrounded Truman when he first arrived in Chicago for the convention seemed to evaporate. Not only had Truman failed to help Harriman, but also he had damaged Stevenson and the party's chances of winning in November.

Truman quickly tried to make amends with Stevenson, campaigning for the nominee but was unable to stem the Eisenhower landslide. After Eisenhower's reelection, Truman again played the role of chronic critic. Just two months after Eisenhower was inaugurated for the second time, Truman was back on the stump. In Topeka, Kansas, he said Eisenhower's state department was guilty of blunders, vacillation, and weakness.

When he was not traveling around the country, he spent his time relaxing at his Independence home. He maintained an office at the Federal Reserve Building in Kansas City.

In 1958, Truman began hammering on a theme which would serve John Kennedy well during the 1960 campaign. Speaking in Chicago, Truman said the United States had fallen behind the Russians in the race for missile supremacy. His attacks against Eisenhower became increasingly personal: Truman said Eisenhower had been a great general, but only because he had someone (Truman) to tell him what to do.

He did not limit himself to criticizing Eisenhower: Truman had something to say on almost any subject. In 1958, he warned that the Capitol dome was in danger of falling over unless the East Front was extended. The next year, he sized up the new Cuban leader, Fidel Castro, and said if Castro "had a haircut and decent clothes he'd be all right."

On foreign affairs, he told students at the University of Wisconsin," I would not trust a Russian across the street. Russia is scared of China. They know they have the yellow death at their back door, and they deserve what they get because they created Red China."

Although Truman had been an early supporter of civil rights, he did not like the movement's growing militancy, believing that civil rights were to be dispensed, not demanded. In 1960, Truman called Martin Luther King, Jr. a troublemaker and later expanded his criticism to the protesters attempting to integrate Southern lunch counters. He said it would not surprise him if they were inspired by communists. His remarks brought criticism from liberals and forced Truman to restate his support of civil rights. While not apologizing for his remarks, he said, "I abhor intolerance in any form. There is no room for it in our Republic. And we cannot deal with race prejudice by high sounding words and pious phrases."

By 1960, Truman was seventy-six and falling further out of touch with a fast-moving world. As the presidential campaign began, Truman went to great lengths to insure that Stevenson would not win a third nomination, calling him indecisive and saying he would be ineffectual as a president. He even wrote an article for *Look* magazine entitled "How Stevenson Let Me Down."

Truman favored his fellow Missourian, Senator Stuart Symington, but his endorsement of Symington came too late to have any impact on the convention. The party would listen to Truman, but would not heed his advice.

When he left the White House, Truman's first concern had been finding a way to earn money. He was offered a job as an executive with an oil company in exchange for $500,000 and a clothing store chain offered him a job as vice-president, but Truman saw clearly that both companies were merely trying to buy his name. He said he would not do anything to capitalize on "The world's most honorable office." He accepted an offer of $600,000 from publisher, Henry Luce, to write his memoirs, which appeared as a book and in *Life* magazine.

In 1958, after nearly a century of consideration, Congress finally passed a presidential pension bill giving former presidents $25,000 a year, plus expenses for postage, office space, and aides. The money from his memoirs, plus the pension and money he received for a series of television shows provided him with a comfortable living.

In 1961, Truman again spoke out on civil rights, saying the Freedom Riders should stay out of the South. Like many Southerners he called the Freedom Riders "outside agitators" who were only stirring up trouble.

Kennedy's election had changed things dramatically for Truman. The Democrats now had a clear leader, and Truman was no longer sought to respond to the actions of a Republican administration. Increasingly, Truman became a kind of presidential ornament. Although his popularity in the White House had declined to record lows, he became remembered not for his acts as president, but for his feisty, fighting style. Kennedy courted him, and when Lyndon Johnson signed the Medicaid legislation, he flew to Missouri to present the first card to Truman. Nixon made his peace with Truman, and Gerald Ford became a big fan, quoting Truman frequently and keeping a bust of the former president in his office. Politics had changed, and presidents no longer said what was on their minds as Truman had done. They said what was safe, but many Americans seemed to yearn for the Truman years when straight speaking was the order of the day.

In 1966, Truman again lashed out at a president, this time criticizing the economic policies of Lyndon Johnson. Truman said that high interest rates could cause a depression. The Vietnam War was becoming a major conflict by 1967, and Truman joined with

Eisenhower to form a committee to support the U.S. effort. The Citizens Committee for Peace With Freedom in Vietnam was designed to counter the growing Vietnam dissent movement. For Truman, the dissent was a replay of the forces that had criticized the Korean War and torn apart his administration. The committee, which grew to more than 100 members, did little, and Truman's involvement was limited almost entirely to lending his name.

He was now in his eighties, and, in 1964, for the first time in more than a quarter of a century, he did not attend the Democratic convention. He spent most of his time in Independence, wrestling with a growing list of health problems.

On December 26, 1972, Truman died in Kansas City of organic failures which caused the collapse of the cardio-vascular system.

Dwight Eisenhower

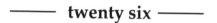

—— twenty six ——

Only three presidents in the twentieth century have served two or more consecutive terms. Woodrow Wilson left the White House near death: his dreams for the League of Nations dead, and his policies rejected by the election of a Republican president. Franklin Roosevelt died in office after serving 12 years. Only Dwight Eisenhower served two full terms and left office with his popularity high. Eisenhower had opposed the constitutional amendment limiting presidents to two terms, but there is no indication that he wanted a third term for himself. He was seventy years old when his term ended and ready to retire to his home in Gettysburg, Pennsylvania.

On his last day as president, he arose at 6:15 in the morning and was at his desk by 7:15 dictating letters. He received his final paycheck, totaling $5,416.69 and an expense check for $2,708.31 He attended John Kennedy's inauguration and left later in the day by car for Gettysburg.

From the moment World War II ended, speculation began about Eisenhower's running for president, but the major question was whether he was a Republican or Democrat. Harry Truman tried to recruit him for the Democrats, but Eisenhower enlisted in the Republican Party. Still he seemed to be almost apolitical while in the White House, never becoming a partisan politician like Harry Truman. After leaving the White House, he became increasingly strident in his pro-Republican leanings and criticisms of the Kennedy Administration.

On June 26, 1961, just five months after his term ended, Eisenhower called for Republican victories in the 1962 Congressional elections and said, "The picture of Government as I see it is of a gigantic Santa Claus and we're dancing around the Christmas tree, hoping for our presents. But each package is marked in fine print so we don't have to read it. 'You won't have to pay for this, but your grandchildren will.'" He told a Pittsburgh audience, "Take back control of your government, take back from the experimenters the planning and the deciding of your country's course. . . ."

Pennsylvania Republicans made a short-lived effort to recruit Eisenhower as a candidate for the U.S. Senate, but he quickly said he had no interest in running for any office again.

Although he lambasted Kennedy's domestic policies (he called the farm policy a monstrosity) Eisenhower refrained from criticizing the Kennedy foreign policy.

From the moment Eisenhower returned to his Gettysburg farm, it became a major tourist attraction. His return came as the nation celebrated the centennial observance of the Civil War, which drew hundreds of thousands of tourists to Gettysburg, many stopping at Eisenhower's home. Eisenhower had Secret Service protection for 30 days after leaving office, but then he was on his own. U.E. Baughman, the chief of the Secret Service, said the tourists were overrunning the Eisenhower farm, even digging up plants to take home as souvenirs. He asked Congress to provide permanent protection for former presidents, but Congress was not ready to take such a step.

He had no worries about money: his autobiography about his years as commander of the Allied armies in World War II had made him a millionaire. After leaving the White House he signed a contract with Doubleday to write a book about his presidency.

Two months after his term ended, Congress granted Eisenhower's wish to return him to his rank as a five-star general. He told friends that he wanted to be called General Eisenhower rather than President Eisenhower.

But he remained very much a politician, working hard for Republican candidates and becoming the leading spokesman for his out-of-power party. Campaigning in New Jersey in 1962, he accused the Democratic candidate for governor of being the tool of the bosses and gave an ominous warning about the future of the major cities, ". . . working men and women suffer under resulting higher taxes, cities and counties wither and the population declines and slums increase. And as industries move away steady and well-paid jobs disappear."

He kept up the pressure on the Kennedy administration, saying Kennedy had surrounded himself with advisors who "treat government as a paradise for theories." For his part, Kennedy kept silent, refusing to respond to Eisenhower's attacks and telling his aides not to exchange charges with the still popular former president. Eisenhower's main criticism of Kennedy centered on the ambitious space program and a plan to provide medical care for the elderly. Eisenhower urged less spending for the space program and dismissed the goal of landing a man on the moon. "Let's find out what is good on earth first."

Eisenhower, like Truman, seemed to be everywhere, speaking on any topic. In Cheyenne, Wyoming, in 1962, he admitted that, "I find myself more deeply involved in this election than any in my experience."

Because he was a former president, he received widespread publicity wherever he spoke, but like Truman, the question was how much control he actually maintained over the party. Truman had learned in 1956 that while he had the attention of the media, he was powerless to stop the nomination of Adlai Stevenson and could not make his own choice more than an also-ran. Eisenhower was clearly alarmed by many of Kennedy's policies and wanted to see him defeated in 1964. He stepped up his criticism following the 1962 elections.

When Kennedy proposed a $100 billion budget for 1964, Eisenhower said it should be reduced by $13 billion, including large cuts in the space program which he called "downright spongy." But the former general also was critical of the buildup in military spending, which Eisenhower said was unnecessary.

When Kennedy was assassinated, Eisenhower was among the mourners at his funeral, but the political ceasefire was short and soon he was back at work urging his party to victory in 1964.

Eisenhower encouraged Henry Cabot Lodge, the 1960 Republican vice-presidential candidate and ambassador to South Vietnam, to run for president. It seemed as though Eisenhower was in the Lodge camp, but a few days later he asked Pennsylvania Governor, William Scranton, to enter the race. Eisenhower wanted a moderate as the party's nominee and was alarmed at the growing strength of Senator Barry Goldwater.

He said he thought Goldwater was impulsive, although he was quick to add that he would be safe for the country. "I doubt that Goldwater would get us into trouble," was far short of an endorsement.

At the 1964 Republican National Convention, Eisenhower was paid $50,000 by the American Broadcasting Company to be an analyst. It was the only starring role he was to play. His influence over the convention was nil. A candidate he did not like, Goldwater, won the nomination. Eisenhower agreed to support the Goldwater ticket, while admitting that it "was not my personal choice." Eisenhower had campaigned everywhere in 1962, but all but sat out the 1964 campaign. He could not bring himself to try to win the presidency for Goldwater.

The Goldwater loss was a debacle for the Republicans, touching off a furious round of finger pointing. Eisenhower held a series of meetings with mainstream Republicans following the election in an attempt to bring the party together again.

A new war was beginning, this time in Vietnam, and once again Eisenhower was enlisted to rally around the flag. Even though as president he had refused to enter Vietnam following the collapse of the French forces in 1954, he now backed U.S. involvement completely. "I do not believe we should quit," he told a Republican gathering in Philadelphia. At the White House he met with Lyndon Johnson and praised the president's Vietnam policy. In 1968, Eisenhower told the Republican Platform Committee that only a show of determination by the United States would force Hanoi to negotiate a peace.

His health was fading, and, in 1968, he was hospitalized at Walter Reed Army Hospital in Washington. He endorsed his old running mate, Richard Nixon, and agreed to speak to the Republican convention via closed-circuit television.

He suffered more heart attacks, his seventh coming in August, and it was clear that it was only a matter of time for the seventy-eight-year-old Eisenhower. On March 28, 1969, his heart finally gave out. He was taken to his boyhood home in Abilene, Kansas, for burial, his funeral train drawing thousands of mourners as it passed from Washington to Abilene.

Eisenhower thought his eight years as president were successful but admitted that he had one major disappointment.

> One of my major regrets is that as we left the White House I had to admit to little success in making progress in global disarmament or in reducing the bitterness of the East-West struggle. . . . I think no one can justifiably charge the bleak record to any lack of striving on our part. . . . But though, in this, I suffered my greatest disappointment, it has not destroyed my faith that in the next generation, the next century, the next millennium these things will come to pass.

Lyndon Johnson

After Lyndon Johnson died, Richard Nixon said, "he thought he could win [his critics]. I think President Johnson died of a broken heart. I really do."

Johnson spent his life accumulating power, relishing it and using it to achieve his goals. He knew that many Americans did not like or trust him: he was too much of a wheeler dealer for them, and his motives were suspect. He tried to win their respect, imploring, lobbying, and at time bullying. Johnson would show the liberals that he was a worthy successor to John F. Kennedy. He pushed through the most impressive package of domestic legislation since his idol, Franklin Roosevelt's, first 100 days. Civil rights bills, legislation to wipe out poverty and cure a score of other social ills sailed through Congress.

In 1964, he was elected in his own right with a resounding mandate, a majority which dwarfed all others. His victory was based in part on his promise to keep U.S. troops out of Vietnam, but it was a promise he would not keep, and it would be his undoing. Johnson had been in the Senate when China fell to the communists, and he had seen the Republicans pillory the Democrats for "losing" China. He would not be the president who lost Vietnam.

The last years of his presidency were a nightmare. He could travel only to military bases without enduring the taunts and violence of the antiwar demonstrators. He wanted desperately to serve another term, a total of nine years as president, second only to Roosevelt, but he knew that even if he won his party's nomination the nation would almost certainly turn against him in the general elections. In March 1968, he announced that he would not be a candidate for reelection. He would leave behind the power he spent a lifetime accumulating.

In the months after his decision, he became withdrawn. Further additions to the Great Society were shelved, and Johnson told aides they could not be passed by a lame-duck president. At times he toyed with the idea that he might yet win his party's nomination and be reelected. He told one aide that Senator James Eastland had urged him to reenter the race, even though Eastland had never before demonstrated any interest in national politics. And so his term ended and he said, "The long, hard effort was over now, and I was glad to see it end," but nobody believed him.

On his relatively small government salary, Johnson had accumulated a vast fortune based on radio and television stations in Texas and large land holdings. In retirement, he would have everything he wanted, except what he wanted most, power.

To the surprise of many, Johnson, the ultimate public man became increasingly private in retirement. He agreed to be interviewed about his presidency for a CBS special shortly after leaving the White House, but generally kept to himself. He refused to grant interviews to reporters he had once hounded with midnight telephone calls. He took an interest in his properties, but only as a diversion.

His intense interest became the building of the Lyndon Johnson Library, the publication of his memoirs, and the development of the LBJ State Park near his Johnson City home. The library would be a huge monument to Johnson and his presidency; his memoirs, for which he was paid $1.2 million, would give him a chance to tell his side.

Johnson talked a great deal about his memoirs, but he had little patience with the discipline required to write a book. He seldom read books and thought it a tiring process. Johnson came upon the idea of recording his recollections and having his assistants use the tapes to write the book. But it did not work: Johnson was best at dealing with people one to one and could not understand how to relate to an audience he could not even see.

The manuscript was dry. Whenever aides attempted to enliven it with some of Johnson's earthy language or true feelings, he protested. At one point, he included a barbed comment about Congressman Wilbur Mills, the chairman of the House Ways and Means Committee. "God damn it, I can't say this, get it out right now, why he may be the speaker of the House someday." Even in retirement, Johnson was aware of power. Later, he said, ". . . for Christ's sake, get that vulgar language of mine out of there. What do you think this is, the tale of an uneducated cowboy? It's a presidential memoir, dammit, and I've got to come out looking like a statesman, not some backwoods politician." The book presented a cardboard man, posturing for history and was by and large a failure.

He tried to rationalize the failure, telling an aide, "All the historians are Harvard people. It just isn't fair. . . . It just isn't fair. Oh, well, why should I care about the future anyhow? I'll be dead then. What matters is now. And I've got exactly what I want right now. . . . I am happy, very happy." But of course he was not.

One rare public moment outside of Texas came in 1969 when he attended the launching of Apollo 11, the first flight to the moon. It was a miserable day that showed him how much power he had lost. He was just one of thousands of dignitaries that day. He sat outside just like the rest, while Vice-President Spiro Agnew received the grand welcome. "I hated being there. I hated people taking pictures of me when I felt so miserable. I hated every minute of it," he told an aide.

He wanted to stay at the ranch, where he could control events, just as he had controlled the nation. He worried over the smallest detail at the ranch, driving through the fields, looking for jobs that needed to be done. Just as he had held meetings with his cabinet and the Joint Chiefs of Staff, he now held daily meetings with the farm foremen. He would lecture them, "Now, I want each of you to make a solemn pledge that you will not go to bed tonight until you are sure that every steer has everything he needs. . . . But it'll mean working every minute of every day."

At night, just as he had read the military reports from Vietnam while president, he read reports about egg production on the ranch and status reports on the cattle. When egg production fell, he investigated. When pump parts were late, he called the president of the pump manufacturing company personally. The company president told him the pumps would be sent that day, and Johnson, sounding like the president of old thanked him "for your help and support at this critical time."

But the parts were delayed in transit, and again Johnson took to the telephone, this time calling the head of American Airlines Air Freight. Not until the pump was delivered was Johnson satisfied.

The LBJ park held a special love for Johnson. Unlike the book, the park gave him a chance to see real people who had come to learn more about him. In her book about Johnson, his aide, Doris Kearns, shows the detail Johnson went to in keeping tabs on the park. He checked the license plates on the visitors' cars to see how many states were represented. He wanted people to come, to see his birthplace, and perhaps better understand him. He required the park employees to file written reports on admissions and postcard sales. When he found that attendance figures did not match admissions he asked why. He was told that some people sent their children in while they waited in the car, or they came up to the house but did not enter. He ordered changes: children would not be allowed in without an adult, and admissions would be collected at the gate, not the house.

Johnson, the multimillionaire, worried about money. He said he had changed the admission policies at the park so that he could increase the pay of the women who worked there. He was worried that adversity would somehow cost him his ranch, just as it had cost his father his land when Johnson was a young man.

To make money, he became an egg salesman. Once a week, he would fly into Austin on a helicopter with a supply of butter and eggs. At his television station, KTBC, he had an announcement made that eggs and butter were for sale in the executive board room, and staffers were able to make their purchases.

Just as he supervised every detail of the ranch and the boyhood home, he presided over the LBJ library. He invited 3,300 of the world's leaders, including President Nixon, to the dedication in 1971. The eight-story library was the largest of the presidential libraries with 31 million papers, compared to just 2 million at the Franklin Roosevelt Library. There were also thousands of books, photographs, and mementos of his life.

Then came a repeat of the events that led to his downfall as president. Johnson began asking for daily attendance figures from the library staff, but they feared his wrath when they were low. So, the staff began to escalate the attendance figures, just as the military had escalated the figures in Vietnam.

He showed little interest in politics, although he did advise some state candidates he favored. He received regular briefings on military affairs from the Nixon White House. Johnson had criticized Hubert Humphrey's 1968 campaign, mainly because Humphrey had not supported Johnson's Vietnam policy. The Democratic candidate in 1972, George McGovern, was even less appealing to Johnson. Still, as a loyal Democrat, he issued a statement endorsing McGovern, although the endorsement was at best lukewarm and pointed to what Johnson called "widely differing opinions" on many issues. McGovern visited Johnson at the ranch, but the former president did little to aid McGovern's campaign.

In April 1972, Johnson suffered a heart attack in Charlottesville, Virginia. He recovered but his health began to decline seriously. On January 22, 1973, just two days after the end of what would have been his second term, Johnson suffered a heart attack while taking an afternoon nap. He called for Secret Service agents, but by the time they arrived he was dead.

The day before, Johnson had learned from President Nixon that a ceasefire had been negotiated for Vietnam.

Richard Nixon

—— **twenty eight** ——

White House Press Secretary, Ronald Zeigler, dismissed it as a third rate burglary, but two years after a group of men broke into the Democratic National Committee headquarters at the Watergate complex in Washington, Richard Nixon was forced from office. On the evening of August 8, 1974, Nixon went on television to announce his resignation, effective at noon the next day. Shortly after 9 A.M. the following morning, the Marine Band played "Hail to the Chief," and Richard Nixon entered the East Room of the White House surrounded by his family.

In a rambling, emotional speech to his staff, Nixon talked about his mother and quoted Teddy Roosevelt. Nixon and his family took a helicopter from the White House lawn to Andrews Air Force Base. As he boarded the helicopter he waved his arms in his familiar way, then he was gone. In 1961, after attending the inauguration of John F. Kennedy, Nixon returned to California aboard a commercial plane, and he talked later of the humiliation he suffered. This time he would leave Washington aboard Air Force One, his resignation timed to become effective when he was over Jefferson City, Missouri.

Aboard Air Force One, he was accompanied by his family and a few aides and the usual Secret Service contingent. Also on board were Nixon's faithful servants and the family parrot. The resignation had come quickly, and there was little time to pack. Nevertheless, Mrs. Nixon had quietly and unknown to her husband packed several boxes with his favorite possessions.

Nixon's plane left Washington at 10:17 A.M.; his presidency had less than two hours remaining, and Vice-President Gerald Ford had the same amount of time to wait before assuming the presidency. As they do whenever there is a change of presidents, the White House staff moved quickly to remove all signs that anyone else had lived there. The pictures of Nixon and his family were quickly removed and new pictures of Gerald Ford went up. In the Oval Office, workers cleaned out Nixon's desk.

At noon, as Ford took the oath of office, Richard Nixon dined on a lunch of prime rib, baked potato, beans, and cheesecake, although he only picked at his food. As the Nixon plane landed at the marine base at El Toro, a crowd of more than 5,000 was on hand. The demonstration, unlike so many during the Nixon Administration, had not been carefully orchestrated by his aides. Some of those were merely curious, but most felt an emotional attachment to Richard Nixon and were truly sorry to see him lose the presidency. Nixon left the plane, and someone in the crowd began singing "God Bless America." Quickly, others took up the refrain and soon the crowd became a mighty chorus.

He told the crowd, ". . . having completed one task does not mean that we will just sit back and enjoy this marvelous California climate and do nothing. . . . I am going to continue to work for peace among all the world. I intend to continue to work for opportunity and understanding among the people in America. . . ."

A marine helicopter carried Nixon from the airport to the San Clemente Coast Guard Station, and Nixon disappeared behind the walls of what had been the Western White House. Nixon quickly began to learn what all former presidents come to know: the trappings of power begin to disappear quickly. In the past, a marine guard in dress whites stood at the front gate of Nixon's home; now he was gone. The Pacific beach in front of the house had been closed for nearly six years by the Secret Service; it became Nixon's private beach, but now it was open to anyone. Nixon spent several days adjusting, calling some friends from the old days, including a number of men like Bob Finch and Herb Klein who had been forced out of his administration.

His small staff was overwhelmed with the telephone calls and the thousands of pieces of mail which flooded in from admirers. At first, aides said Nixon was taking the resignation well, but his mood was subject to quick and dramatic changes. He faced both personal and financial disaster, and the resignation had not come close to ending his ordeal. Aides described Nixon as lonely and depressed; at times he would rummage through the piles of unanswered mail or play the piano.

His top aides had already been indicted, and the grand jury had been anxious to indict Nixon at the same time, settling instead for naming Nixon an unindicted coconspirator. The grand jury had been restrained only by Special Prosecutor Leon Jaworski, who did not want to indict a sitting president. Now there was no reason not to indict Nixon.

Nixon still had friends in the White House, led by his former chief of staff Alexander Haig, now a key Ford aide, and there was also Ford himself, the faithful loyalist who had always done Nixon's bidding. Haig, along with other Nixon friends, orchestrated a campaign to win a pardon for Nixon, over the protests of the Ford loyalists, who predicted it would be disastrous for the new president.

On Sunday morning, one month after Nixon's resignation, Ford attended church, then returned to the White House to call key congressmen to inform them of his decision to pardon Nixon. At 11 A.M., the camera crews came into the Oval Office, and Ford began to read his statement. Richard Nixon had his pardon.

Originally, the plan called for Nixon to make a statement of contrition in exchange for his pardon, but his statement was little more than an apology. He admitted no wrongdoing on his part, only that he had failed to act "more decisively and forthrightly in dealing with Watergate. . . ." He admitted mistakes and misjudgments, but that was all. The pardon saved Nixon from criminal prosecution but ruined the Ford administration. Overnight, his popularity dropped more than 20 points in the Gallup Poll.

Even though he had admitted no criminal conduct, Nixon was troubled by accepting the pardon. It did little to improve his mood, and an old leg ailment had flared anew. For more than a decade, Nixon had suffered from phlebitis, which caused swelling in his leg. Phlebitis can be fatal. The swelling is caused by a clot in the leg, and if the clot should break free and block an artery, it can cause death.

His doctors urged him to enter a hospital for treatment, but at first Nixon refused. Finally, they convinced him to check into Long Beach Memorial Hospital. There was no doubt that Nixon needed the medical attention, but many Americans were suspicious. The trial of John Mitchell, Bob Haldeman, and John Ehrlichman was getting underway in Washington and Nixon had been subpoenaed to testify. Many suspected that his medical condition was merely an attempt to avoid appearing in court to testify in a criminal trial.

Nixon was released from the hospital after undergoing tests and allowed to return home to rest. His leg still caused pain, but he was more troubled by his financial plight. His property in Florida and California gave him a net worth of more than two million dollars, yet his cash flow was precarious. Following the pardon, a vindictive Congress had slashed the $850,000 requested for transition money. His legal bills would total nearly half a million dollars and items that had been paid for by the federal government—such as care of the grounds at Nixon's home—were now his responsibility.

A Nixon attorney, Dean Butler, told reporters Nixon was nearly broke, the result of the legal fees and an inability to commit himself to money-making projects because of distractions. At one point, Nixon's checking balance fell to just $500.

His financial salvation came from Warner Books, which offered Nixon a $2.5 million advance for his memoirs, plus a guarantee to pay all expenses above $300,000. The money would be paid to Nixon as the book progressed. Nixon's financial problems were solved, although the grounds soon looked like an overgrown vacant lot, and a local Boy Scout troop was enlisted to trim the weeds. A group of volunteers were also recruited to begin answering the mail that had piled up.

On October 23, Nixon's doctors examined his leg again and found that despite the medication to reduce the swelling, his condition had not improved. He was readmitted to the hospital, and new tests showed that a main vein was almost completely blocked by a clot. Surgery was necessary, even vital, to save Nixon's life. The surgery was a relatively simple procedure, and Nixon was soon back in his hospital room to recuperate.

Early in the afternoon, a nurse checked on Nixon's condition and found him unconscious. The nurse shouted at Nixon, then slapped his face, but failed to gain a response. Nixon had slipped into shock. The drugs designed to reduce the blood clots had also caused internal bleeding, and Nixon had lost a great deal of blood. It took the doctors three hours to stabilize his condition and save his life. He remained on the critical list until November 3 and was released 11 days later. His illness did convince Judge John Sirica that Nixon was in no shape to testify at the criminal trial in Washington. On New Year's Day, Haldeman, Ehrlichman, and Mitchell were found guilty.

Nixon had become a recluse behind the walls of his estate. He had failed to purchase private health insurance after leaving the White House and had $23,000 in medical bills to pay.

Although safe from criminal prosecution, more than 30 suits had been filed against Nixon, and he needed more money to pay his lawyers. A curious character, Rabbi Baruch Korff had become a Nixon supporter following the Watergate break in and gradually grew closer to Nixon. After the resignation, Korff became more important than ever, raising money to pay Nixon's growing legal bills. Korff loved the media attention; he would meet with Nixon, then brief reporters on what he had seen and heard. He was able to raise more than $100,000 before withdrawing for unknown reasons.

Nixon sold his Key Biscayne, Florida, home for a profit of more than one million dollars, and he began to have second thoughts about his decision to live in California. The house was isolated and clearly out of the mainstream. The grounds were difficult to care for and weeds began to dominate the once well-manicured lawn.

February 9, 1975 marked the six-month anniversary of Nixon's resignation. It was more than a milestone: it marked the end of Nixon's transition money, and he was forced to let several staff members, including Zeigler, go. His direct line with the White House was removed and his few remaining trappings of power disappeared. He hit upon another money-making plan, this one inspired by his former aide Bob Haldeman.

Haldeman had been paid $100,000 by CBS for an interview. If Haldeman was worth $100,000, Nixon wondered, how much would an interview with the former president be worth. CBS had drawn much criticism for paying for the Haldeman interview and was not interested in the Nixon interview. ABC said no, but NBC said it would be willing to pay $300,000 for an interview. Then, British television personality David Frost bid $600,000 plus 20 percent of the profits for 4, 90 minute interviews with Nixon.

Frost put together his own network of 145 stations in the United States, and sold rights in 14 other nations. The interviews were hardly journalistic triumphs, but they drew large audiences, and both Frost and Nixon made a small fortune.

The memoirs were going slowly and finally Warner Books sold part of the rights to another publisher in hopes that it would have better luck in speeding up the work.

Late in 1975, Nixon began to emerge from his self-imposed exile. In a story for the *Ladies Home Journal,* he said the United States was a compromised country in need of restoring its pride. As for Ford, the man who had paid a terrible political price for pardoning Nixon, the former president said, "He's okay."

In 1972, Nixon had reopened ties with China in an historic trip to Peking. The Chinese had never understood Watergate and held Nixon in high regard. Almost from the moment he resigned, the Chinese had begun inviting Nixon to return to Peking. Nixon finally decided to go to China in late February, 1976. The departure came just three days before the crucial New Hampshire primary where Ford was in a tight race with Ronald Reagan. The trip proved to be a major embarrassment to Ford.

In 1978, Nixon's memoirs were published, generally drawing poor reviews, but selling well. The book, *RN,* was on the best seller list for more than three months. Soon after the publication of his memoirs, he signed a contract to write a book about the challenges facing the nation.

Except for gatherings with friends, Nixon had avoided making public appearances in the United States. Late in 1978, the community of Hayden, Kentucky, completed construction on a recreation center, paid for with $2.7 million in federal money. Originally, it was hoped that Gerald Ford would attend the dedication ceremonies and in return have the center named for him. But Ford could not attend, and so, the town decided to invite Nixon and name it in his honor. Nixon accepted the offer immediately. It was almost as though he had not been forced to resign in disgrace four years earlier; thousands of people turned out, some carrying signs reading "Nixon's the One—in 1980," and wearing "I Like Nixon" buttons. There was a motorcade and a well-received speech by Nixon. There were some small problems; the anticipated crowd of 40,000 turned out to be 10,000, and an Army band refused to appear when the hosts demanded that "Hail to the Chief" be played (the anthem is reserved for sitting presidents), and a four-piece high school board was recruited to play the song twice.

In 1980, Nixon moved to New York, buying a townhouse for $750,000. In 1962, after losing the election for governor of California, Nixon moved to New York to make a fresh start, remaining there until he became president. This time, he stayed for just one year before buying a $1.2 million house in New Jersey. He sold his New York City home for $2.9 million.

He wrote a third book and became more accessible. In 1981, he gave an interview to a Miami radio station and talked about the Miami Dolphins, but still he would not admit guilt for Watergate. A 1982 survey showed that 56 percent of those surveyed felt that Nixon should have gone on trial for his role in Watergate and 47 percent still believed Ford was wrong to pardon Nixon. Three out of four said Nixon was guilty of wrongdoing and took part in Watergate.

But he was now sought; journalists who had called for his resignation now sought interviews, and some politicians even sought his endorsement. There were still embarrassments. Duke University (where Nixon received his law degree in 1937) said it was not interested in being the home to a Nixon library, and protesters still showed up when he made a speech. The Republican party all but ignored him officially: his name was not mentioned at the party's 1976 and 1980 conventions.

Behind the scenes, he gave advice to both Gerald Ford and Ronald Reagan, although his first choice for president, John Connally, failed to catch fire with the voters.

From the day Nixon left office, his lawyers began fighting for possession of millions of documents from his administration. Since the administration of George Washington, the government had always assumed that presidents owned the papers from their administration. After Nixon was forced to resign, Congress passed the Presidential Recordings and Materials Preservation Act and took control of Nixon's papers. What proved particularly embarrassing for Nixon were the tape recordings made in the Oval Office. They revealed Nixon plotting the Watergate coverup. In 1980, the National Archives began offering the public a chance to hear some of the most incriminating recordings.

Nixon's standing in the United States might have fallen, but he remained popular around the world, especially in countries where corruption is viewed as an acceptable part of government. Gregory Arbatov, a member of the Soviet Communist Party's Central Committee, said in 1983 that the Soviets considered Nixon to be the most effective postwar president.

He spoke to students at Oxford University and made a second trip to China. When he went to the funeral of Anwar Sadat, he skipped the return flight with other members of the United State delegation to visit Saudi Arabia.

In 1984, CBS purchased a series of interviews with Nixon conducted by his former aide and speech writer Frank Gannon. The network paid $500,000 for the interviews, although it is unknown how much Nixon received. His second and third books, like his first, received generally poor reviews, but Nixon had predicted that they would, and the reviews did not seem to bother him.

After ten years, Richard Nixon had returned. He talked of living to see the start of the twenty-first century, when he would be eighty-seven years old. But as he constantly told friends, he was still the only American citizen over the age of 35 who could not run for president.

Gerald Ford

—— twenty nine ——

At first, it did not occur to former presidents to capitalize on the presidency. Later, presidents such as Calvin Coolidge and Harry Truman did use their former office to make money, but they seemed almost embarrassed and even issued statements promising to do nothing to compromise the presidency. Gerald Ford, the only man to become president without being elected either president or vice-president, has traded on his former office to enrich himself in almost every possible way.

Not since Franklin D. Roosevelt took office in the midst of the Depression has a president taken the leadership of the nation under worse conditions. President Richard Nixon, facing certain impeachment by the Congress, resigned on August 9, 1974, turning over the presidency to Ford. During the two previous years, the nation had been consumed by the Watergate scandal. Ford, the House minority leader and a Nixon loyalist, was named vice-president after Spiro Agnew was forced to resign in a separate scandal involving tax fraud and bribery.

Ford's 30 months as president were undistinguished, and in 1976 he was defeated by Jimmy Carter. The election was close: a few thousand votes the other way could have given the victory to Ford. When candidates lose by a landslide, there are few second thoughts, but when the election is close, the loser agonizes over what might have been. For Ford, the issue was his decision to pardon Nixon.

As a congressman, Ford had lived in a middle-class neighborhood. The presidency introduced Ford to a new life style, enabling

him to make friends with men who would have barely acknowledged him when he was a congressman.

Before his appointment to the vice-presidency, Ford had planned his retirement—a modest retirement on a congressman's pension. After his forced retirement by the voters, Ford decided to retire to Palm Springs, California, home of some of the nation's wealthiest men who shared his political philosophy.

Ford plunged into a series of money-making activities, and
soon his annual income approached one million dollars and by
1984 his net worth was estimated at more than six million dollars.
His wealthy friends helped him find business opportunities.
Leonard Firestone brought him in as a partner in the purchase of
two radio stations in Colorado, where Ford owned a ski chalet.
Eight companies named Ford to their board of directors, largely as
an ornament. One company, 20th Century Fox, paid Ford $50,000 a
year for serving on its board.

Ford also hit the lecture circuit, giving some 30 speeches a year
for fees ranging from $10,000 to $15,000. He also became an inves-
tor in a controversial $90 million resort development near Palm
Springs. To overcome opposition to the project, Ford was enlisted
by the developers as a spokesman and lobbyist.

In Palm Springs, the city named a street for Ford near Bob
Hope Drive and Frank Sinatra Drive. The city is a center for show
business performers, and gradually Ford became a performer,
signing a contract to appear on NBC and even making an appearance on the television show "Dynasty."

Surrounded by friends in the type of environment Palm
Springs creates, almost anything begins to seem possible. In 1980,
it briefly seemed possible for Ford to make a comeback, to recapture the White House. In 1977, Ford began making appearances for
Republican candidates, gathering political chips he could play in
another presidential campaign. Ronald Reagan was preparing for
another try at the White House and collecting the same kind of
political IOUs.

Unlike Reagan, Ford hesitated. His friends, perhaps seeing a
chance to return to power, urged him on, but by the time Ford
began to enter the race it was too late. In early 1980, with primary
deadlines in some states past and the first delegates selected, aides
to Ford floated stories about his probable interest in the race.

But reality soon set in, and even before he was officially in the race, Ford was out. He disliked Reagan, blaming him for dividing the party in 1976 through bitter primaries, but his dislike of Jimmy Carter was even greater. Ford endorsed Reagan to get revenge on Carter.

In July of 1980, one of the most unusual events in American politics occurred at the Republican National Convention. Ford, in an interview with television anchorman, Walter Cronkite, said he might be willing to accept the vice-presidential nomination and run with Reagan. But in his negotiations with Reagan, Ford made it clear that he did not want to be an ordinary vice-president whose duties are decided by the whim of the president.

Ford wanted to serve as a kind of chief operating officer in a re-structured White House organization. He would have control over national security issues, and the presidency would be shared by two men. As Ford's list of demands grew longer, Reagan began to resist, even though the delegates were calling a Reagan-Ford combination a dream ticket. The negotiations broke down and Reagan chose George Bush as his vice-presidential nominee. In a Detroit hotel room, Ford's political career came to an end.

In the presidential campaign, Ford did more for Reagan than Reagan had ever done for Ford in the 1976 campaign. He spoke in 30 states, covering nearly 60,000 miles, repeating the message that Carter must be defeated. His motives were clear when he said in an interview, "He [Carter] misled and deceived the American people in the 1976 campaign. And now the chickens are coming home to roost. . . . He's going to be held to account."

Reagan won the election, and Ford returned to Palm Springs and his business ventures. One money-making scheme was a sharp break with presidential tradition. Ford agreed to promote a series of medals manufactured by the Franklin Mint, a private man-ufacturer of collectibles. For an undisclosed fee, Ford agreed to pro-mote the medals and help prepare the advertising.

He spent much of his time raising money for a museum and li-brary to house his papers and memorabilia in his hometown of Grand Rapids. A committee raised $11.5 million for the building with one million dollars coming from the government of Japan, $200,000 from Saudi Arabia, and $100,000 from the Shah of Iran. It included a reproduction of the Oval Office and of the quonset hut that served as Ford's headquarters when he first ran for Congress in 1946.

Under federal law, presidents are required to raise the necessary money to build their library, then the government pays for maintaining it. Presidential libraries are a product of the modern presidency: the first was built by Herbert Hoover. Presidents such as Woodrow Wilson and George Washington simply turned their papers over to the Library of Congress. Increasingly, the libraries have become huge monuments to the former presidents, and the cost to the taxpayers has increased to millions of dollars a year.

Once Carter was out of the White House, Ford's attitude toward his political enemy began to mellow and they joined forces to encourage voter registration.

Presidents are limited in what they can say on certain controversial issues. A misstatement can cost the support of a large block of voters. One such issue is the debate over whether the United States should talk directly with representatives of the Palestine Liberation Organization. President after president, including Ford and Carter, have promised that the United States would never negotiate with the PLO.

Following the assassination of Egyptian President Anwar Sadat, Nixon and Carter immediately announced plans to attend his funeral. For security reasons, President Reagan and Vice-President Bush decided not to attend the funeral. Secretary of State Alexander Haig suggested that since Nixon and Carter were already going, the addition of Ford would make a most impressive delegation. The three men arrived in Washington with two things in common; they were former presidents, and they had been rejected: Ford and Carter in elections and Nixon through a forced resignation.

They were wary of each other at first. Finally Ford broke the ice, suggesting a treaty for the length of their trip: if they could not be friendly, they could be cordial.

After attending the funeral, Nixon left quickly for a trip to Saudi Arabia and Ford and Carter returned to the United States. On board the plane, they broke with their past policies and said the United States should be willing to talk with the PLO as a way of advancing Middle East peace prospects. The Reagan administration, aware of the political damage such a stand could cause, politely ignored their advice.

Ford may represent a new kind of former president or merely an aberration. A man who uses his former position as a vehicle to become wealthy and who speaks to almost any group as long as the money is right, Ford, like Nixon before him, and Carter after him, hired a theatrical agent to handle negotiations for television and personal appearances. Although Ford has made more public appearances than any other former president, he is one of the least listened to. Ford may have shown that a former president can gain wealth without gaining respect.

Jimmy Carter

—— thirty ——

Jimmy Carter came to Washington in 1977 as an outsider and left four years later the same way. From the beginning, he had been unable to gain control of the levers that run the government, and in the end the voters turned him out. The defeat was so total that there was no doubt that Carter could not even attempt a comeback; his political career was over.

Carter returned to his home in Plains, Georgia, a small town that had undergone dramatic changes in the previous four years. After Carter's election, the town became a mecca for tourists; the small shops along Main Street filled up with souvenirs and at one time five separate companies operated tour buses taking tourists past such sites as Billy Carter's gas station, Miss Lillian's home, and of course Carter's house.

As Carter's popularity faded, so did the tourists. The shops were still filled with trinkets, but there were few customers. The five tour companies folded, but there were still reminders of the heady years. The Taiwan government gave $25,000 for a park, Chinese Air Lines donated a large aluminum eagle, and, in a bid for publicity, the failing World Team Tennis league built two tennis courts.

The police department expanded from one night watchman to a six-man force. After Carter's return, the force was cut to two officers. Almost from the moment he returned to Plains, Carter began speaking out. In March, he began calling members of Congress to lobby against budget cuts proposed by President Ronald Reagan.

He also enlisted his former aides to fight the proposed cuts. Later in the month he went public with his criticisms, but his impact was minimal. Carter's presidency had become synonymous with failure. Speaking to students at Princeton University, even Carter admitted that he was not as effective as he wanted to be and might have been more forceful with Iran following the takeover of the U.S. Embassy in Tehran.

After leaving the White House, Carter told friends that he thought it was inappropriate for Gerald Ford to be engaged in so many money-making ventures. And yet his reservations about Ford did not stop Carter from signing a contract worth nearly two million for his memoirs. Carter also hired an agent, Norman Brokaw of the William Morris Agency. Brokaw saw unlimited possibilities for Carter and his wife Rosalynn. "If he and Mrs. Carter appear as a double, they can probably get $25,000 a night. They can be the first presidential husband and wife act in history," Brokaw said. The nation had moved from Thomas Jefferson struggling to pay his bills to the husband and wife team of Carter and Carter.

In 1981, he toured China and Japan. He joked with Chinese Vice-Chairman Deng Xiaoping saying that if Deng had been his running mate he would have won reelection. In his own mind, Carter was sure why he lost the election. He did not blame the man who defeated him, but what he referred to as the two "K's", Kennedy and Khomeini.

He had wasted too much time fending off the Kennedy challenge in the Democratic primaries, and he called Ayatollah Ruhollah Khomeini, "unpredictable, weak in a time of crisis." Carter could not admit that many Americans viewed him as the one who was unpredictable and weak. In October, 1981, Carter moved back onto the front pages. The *Washington Post* reported that in the final days of his presidency, Carter had bugged the Blair House where Ronald Reagan was staying. Carter threatened to sue, and the *Post* retracted its story and apologized.

Carter worked on his memoirs, entitled "Keeping Faith." The reviewers found it naive and dull. Some complained that Carter had taken credit for every success while shifting the blame for failures to others. As part of Carter's deal, Rosalynn Carter also wrote a book, which turned out to be both more informative and better received than her husband's book.

Carter made a handful of political speeches, but he was ignored by the party until 1984. Walter Mondale, Carter's vice-president, had spent three years trying to put as much distance as possible between himself and Carter. But Mondale desperately needed Carter's help in the South, especially Georgia.

Although Carter was invited to the 1984 Democratic convention, and despite Mondale's plea for help, Carter remained an outsider in his party. He had joined Nixon and Lyndon Johnson on the list of former presidents their parties did not like to mention.

Bibliography

Anderson, Judith Icke. *William Howard Taft, An Intimate History.* W.W. Norton, New York, 1981.

Barnard, Harry. *Rutherford B. Hayes and His America.* Bobbs-Merrill, Indianapolis, 1954.

Bemis, Samuel Flagg. *John Quincy Adams and the Union.* Alfred Knopf, New York, 1956.

Brant, Irving. *The Fourth President, A Life of James Madison.* Bobbs-Merrill, Indianapolis, 1970.

Buchanan, James. *Mr. Buchanan's Administration on the Eve of the Rebellion.* Appleton, New York, 1866.

Burner, David. *Herbert Hoover, A Public Life.* Alfred A. Knopf, New York, 1979.

Busch, Noel F. *TR, The Story of Theodore Roosevelt and His Influence on our Times.* Reynal Company, New York, 1963.

Chambers II, John Whiteclay. "Presidents Emeritus." *American Heritage, 30,* June 1979, pp. 16–25.

Clark, Bennett Champ. *John Quincy Adams, Old Man Eloquent.* Little, Brown, Boston, 1932.

Cochran, Bert. *Harry Truman and the Crisis Presidency.* Funk & Wagnalls, New York, 1973.

Donovan, Robert J. *Tumultuous Years, The Presidency of Harry S. Truman, 1949–1953.* W.W. Norton, New York, 1982.

Dozer, Donald M. "Benjamin Harrison and the Presidential Campaign of 1892." *American Historical Review, 54,* Oct. 1948, pp. 49–77.

Flexner, James Thomas. *George Washington, Anguish and Farewell, 1793–1799.* Little, Brown, Boston, 1972.

Ford, Gerald. *A Time to Heal.* Harper & Row, New York, 1979.

Fuess, Claude M. *Calvin Coolidge, The Man from Vermont.* Little, Brown, Boston, 1940.

Grant, Ulysses S. *Personal Memoirs of U.S. Grant.* C.L. Webster, New York, 1885–1886, 2 vols.

Harbaugh, William Henry. *Power and Responsibility: The Life and Times of Theodore Roosevelt.* Farrar, Strauss, and Cudahy, New York, 1961.

Harrison, Benjamin. *This Country of Ours.* Scribner, New York, 1897.

Hecht, Marie B. *John Quincy Adams, A Personal History of an Independent Man.* Macmillan, New York, 1972.

Hesseltine, William B. *Ulysses S. Grant, Politician.* Dodd, New York, 1935.

Howe, George Frederick. *Chester A. Arthur: A Quarter-Century of Machine Politics.* Dodd, Mead, New York, 1934.

Hoyt, Edwin. *Martin Van Buren.* Reilly & Lee, Chicago, 1964.

James, Marquis. *Andrew Jackson, Portrait of a President.* Bobbs-Merrill, Indianapolis, 1937.

Kane, Joseph Nathan. *Facts about the Presidents.* H.W. Wilson, New York, 1959.

Kearns, Dorris. *Lyndon Johnson & The American Dream.* Harper & Row, New York, 1976.

Klein, Philip Shriver. *President James Buchanan, A Biography.* Pennsylvania State University Press, University Park, 1962.

Kurtz, Stephen G. *The Presidency of John Adams: The Collapse of Federalism.* University of Pennsylvania Press, Philadelphia, 1957.

Lorant, Stefan. *The Life and Times of Theodore Roosevelt.* Doubleday, Garden City, New York, 1959.

Lyon, Peter. *Eisenhower, Portrait of the Hero.* Little, Brown, Boston, 1974.

McFeely, William S. *Grant, A Biography.* W.W. Norton, New York, 1981.

McKinley, Silan B. *Woodrow Wilson, A Biography.* Praeger, New York, 1957.

McKitrick, Eric L. *Andrew Johnson and Reconstruction.* University of Chicago Press, Chicago, 1960.

Malone, Dumas. *Jefferson and His Times, The Sage of Monticello.* Little, Brown, Boston, 1981.

Martin, Asa E. *After the White House,* Penns Valley Publishers, State College, Pa., 1951.

Miller, Merle. *Lyndon, An Oral Biography.* Putnam, New York, 1980.

_____. *Plain Speaking, An Oral Biography of Harry S. Truman.* Putnam's, New York, 1973.

Mowry, George E. *Theodore Roosevelt and the Progressive Movement.* Hill and Wang, New York, 1946.

Myers, Elisabeth O. *Benjamin Harrison.* Reilly & Lee, Chicago, 1969.

Nagel, Paul C. *Descent from Glory, Four Generations of the John Adams Family.* Oxford University Press, New York, 1983.

Nevins, Allan. *Grover Cleveland, A Story in Courage.* Dodd, Mead, New York, 1932.

Nichols, Roy F. *Franklin Pierce, Young Hickory of the Granite Hills.* University of Pennsylvania Press, Philadelphia, 1958.

Niven, John. *Martin Van Buren.* Oxford University Press, New York, 1983.

Polk, James K. *The Diary of a President.* Edited by Allan Nevins. Longman's Green, New York.

Pringle, Henry F. *Theodore Roosevelt, A Biography.* Harcourt, Brace, New York, 1931.

Rayback, Robert J. *Millard Fillmore, Biography of a President.* Buffalo Historical Society, Buffalo, 1959.

Reeves, Thomas C. *Gentleman Boss, The Life of Chester Arthur.* Alfred A. Knopf, New York, 1975.

Rosebloom, Eugene H. *A History of Presidential Elections.* Macmillan, New York, 1959.

Schachner, Nathan. *Thomas Jefferson.* Thomas Yoseloff, New York, 1957.

Seager II, Robert. *And Tyler Too.* McGraw-Hill, New York, 1963.

Sellers, Charles Grier. *James K. Polk, Jacksonian.* Princeton University Press, Princeton, N.J., 1957.

Sievers, Harry J. *Benjamin Harrison.* Bobbs-Merrill, Indianapolis, 1968.

Smith, Gene. *The Shattered Dream.* William Morrow, New York, 1970.

_____. *When the Cheering Stopped.* William Morrow, New York, 1964.

Smith, Page. *John Adams.* Doubleday, Garden City, N.Y., 1962, 2 vols.

Steinberg, Alfred. *The Man from Missouri, The Life and Times of Harry S. Truman.* G.P. Putnam's Sons: New York, 1962.

Thane, Elswyth. *Potomac Squire.* Duell, Sloan & Pearce, New York, 1963.

Thomas, Lately. *The First President Johnson.* William Morrow, New York, 1968.

Tugwell, Rexford. *Grover Cleveland.* MacMillan, New York, 1968.

Walworth, Arthur. *Woodrow Wilson.* Houghton Mifflin, Boston, 1965.

Ward, John William. *Andrew Jackson, Symbol for an Age.* Oxford University Press, New York, 1955.

Warren, Harris G. *Herbert Hoover and the Great Depression.* Oxford University Press, New York, 1959.

Whitney, David C. *The American Presidents.* Doubleday, Garden City, N.Y., 1978.

Wilmerding, Lucius. *James Monroe, Public Claimant.* Reuters University Press, New Brunswick, N.J., 1960.

Index

About the Author

James C. Clark is deputy managing editor of *The Orlando Sentinel.* His coverage of government has won numerous honors, including The George Polk Award, The Sigma Delta Chi Award, and The Gerald Loeb Award. His work has appeared in *The Washington Post, Washington Monthly, The Nation* and *Civil War Times.* Before joining *The Sentinel,* he worked for The Associated Press, United Press International, *The Tampa Tribune* and *The Raleigh News & Observer.*

Clark lives in Orlando, Florida with his wife Jane and son Randall.